Love not Fear:

a new paradigm for the 21st century

ISBN: 9798621037062 - This is a Towards Utopia Movement publication (c) 2018. Please give this book away to everyone you know. There is a modest fee for the Kindle and paperback versions but the PDF version is free. If you are reading the Kindle or paperback version please also download the PDF version from https://lovenotfear.uk/FreeGift.php and give that away free. If you are in business you may give it to your customers, include it in a bundle you are selling or offer it as a free inducement. The important thing is to get this message out to the world. The only condition is that you do not change this book in any way. Thank you.

Contents:

CHAPTER ONE - Love not Fear

"The ancient Greeks had a legend that all things were created by love. Everyone was happy because love was everywhere. All vide with the other to make those around him happy. Then one night while love slept, fear crept in and with it came disease and lack and unhappiness for where love attracts, fear repels. Love gives freely while fear is afraid that there will not be enough, so holds on to everything it has."

from The Magic Word by Robert Collier.

But a better way is possible.

Just imagine how much better life would be if we no longer lived in fear, if we no longer made each other afraid.

Just imagine how much higher we could all live if, instead of doing each other down, we all helped raise each other up.

How much richer we could all be, how much happier, how much safer we could all feel.

Hurt people hurt people and frightened people threaten and intimate people.

Wouldn't it be great if we no longer lived in fear?

Wouldn't it be great if we were all excellent to each other?

It's the 21st century FFS! Isn't it about time we stopped living by the law of the jungle and started living by the law of love?

Every day we are presented with choices. Every day we get to choose whether to move the world a little bit closer to hell or heaven, to utopia or dystopia. It's our choice.

When we see someone struggling, we can help him up or we can see an opportunity to gain at his expense. It's up to us.

Ask yourself "what kind of world do I want to live in?" Choose wisely.

Can we please help each other more and try not to hurt or scare anyone.

A better way is possible.

We live on such a beautiful planet. Life should be glorious, yet many of us are not experiencing that glory.

If only we could live together in peace. If only we could all care for each-other. If only we could find a way to overcome our fears and our egos. If only we could be excellent to each-other and spread our love, then we

2

really could experience the glory of living in Utopia.

So what's stopping us? In this controversial book I examine some of the obstacles in our way and suggest strategies for moving forward, together, into the glorious future we all deserve.

Come with me on this journey and let's build that utopian world together by being excellent to each other and spreading our love.

Thank you for reading this little book. May it bring much love and joy into your life. Please share it with as many friends and colleagues as possible. It is a great little book.

Please give this book away to everyone you know. There is a modest fee for the Kindle version but the PDF version is free. If you are reading the Kindle version please also download the PDF version from https://lovenotfear.uk/FreeGift.php and give that away free. If you are in business you may give it to your customers, include it in a bundle you are selling or offer it as a free inducement. The important thing is to get this message out to the world. The only condition is that you do not change this book in any way. Thank you.

I have a dream of a future world where there is no more war because everyone loves and respects each other, each other's national boarders and each other's national cultures.

Where we no longer invade other nations to depose their leaders and impose Rothschild owned central banks upon them.

Where we are more interested in what we can give than in what we can get.

Where we all make sure our neighbours, as well of people on the other side of the world, always have enough .

Where there is tolerance and free speech. Where you don't have to agree with what people are saying in order to stand up for their right to say it. Where people don't need to walk around on eggshells to avoid *offending* intolerant people.

Where politicians are controlled by the people, not the other way around.

Where people don't need governments to make them do what is right but where joint policy decisions are made by a truly representative democratic process.

In short, a world where everyone loves and is excellent to one and other.

You may say I'm a dreamer but I'm not the only one.

This world is broken.

Everything about it is broken. The very basis of our

society and of our economic system is broken. The trouble is that its all been broken for so long that everyone thinks its normal. I do wonder what a visitor from another planet would make of us. I know what I make of us and its not polite. Now I'm certainly not claiming to be from another planet (despite what some of you might think) but I can see a better, more loving way forward. Perhaps you will share my vision, or maybe not, that's your choice and I respect it, but please do read my little book with an open mind before deciding.

If we were all excellent to eachother there would be no poverty. If we saw someone worse off than ourselves we would give them a little of what we had. We wouldn't need to give them very much because everyone in the area would be giving them something. They would be back on their feet in no time. But it doesn't happen like that. Why?

Two reasons. The first cause is that there are selfish, greedy people in the world, sure there are, but most of us are good, decent folk. But the good, decent people, many of them, most of the time, ignore the poverty and suffering of others too. There must be a second cause. What is it? I believe that it is fear. We live in a world of fear, mostly fear of poverty and debt. We fear we may lose our job or our business, that we will no longer be able to service our credit card debt or our mortgage. If we were not living in fear ourselves we would be much quicker to help others.

The irony of this old, worn out paradigm, of our old,

worn out culture of fear, is that if we did all help one and other, we would be confident others would help us too and there would be no more fear. And being free of fear we would be free to help eachother. So the remedy to the problem lies in our own hands. Each and every one of us can start today to help others more.

The rich globalist elite thrive on our fear. They use our fear as a tool to sell us goods we don't need, shipped from the other side of the planet, paid for on credit we can't afford . They use fear to make us vote at election time for dishonest politicians who are more a part of the problem than of the solution. They use fear to keep us as debt slaves, working for fifty years at jobs where we have little control, to pay for the right to live on our own planet.

There really is a sucker born every minute and those suckers are us, every one of us. Actually more than 200,000 new suckers are born every single day (that the net figure, 360,000 babies are born every day and 151,600 people die). 200,000 more debt slaves for the rich, globalist elite. Just let that sink in for a moment, just for a moment.

If we really loved them we would not permit them to become debt slaves but what can we do about it?

A Game We Did Not Devise

We are born into a game we did not devise where the rules are stacked against us and in favour of the globalist elite. We have no way to win this game. We may make some money, we may get a fancy job title, we may even get some power but ultimately, even as the CEO of a big company, we can never win this game. There will always be a bigger parasite sucking us dry. Our only way out is to stop playing this game and devise a fairer one.

The currency of the game is money. Stop using money and the game is over. The banks will collapse. The globalist elite will be reduced to ordinary citizens, just like us. The nightmare game will be over and we will be free.

We will be free to devise a new game based on freely giving and freely receiving, on helping each other to thrive, on freedom and independence and on love and co-operation. A true loving utopia.

It is my true belief that the thing that makes people mean, intolerant and aggressive is fear, fear of poverty, fear of attack by individuals, terrorists or foreign powers, fear of death or the even greater fear of living a meaningless life.

We feel threatened so we threaten and attack others.

There is a well known saying that *hurt people hurt people*. Well let's add to that *threatened people threaten people* and *invaded people invade people*.

We invade other people's countries then wonder why their terrorists attack us. We are mean to our workers then blame them for going on strike. Some intolerant migrants call our women *white prostitutes* for dressing normally then wonder why our people are intolerant of their dress choice.

But wouldn't it be wonderful if nobody felt threatened anymore, if we all felt safe and appreciated? Wouldn't that be a better world to live in?

This is a very controversial book and I don't expect you will all agree with everything I say, and that's okay. This next little bit is probably the most controversial of all. Please take from it what you will and leave the rest. That's okay too.

In this book I talk a lot about being excellent to *each-other* and I talk about *other people* but I don't really believe there are any other people to complain about or to be excellent to. Let me explain

You have probably heard it said before that *we are all one*. That idea can be taken on many different levels. We can talk about the *brotherhood of man* or whatever the modern politically correct version of that may be. Some people, such as myself, take the idea further. We believe it to be literately true.

Think of a group of islands in a warm sea somewhere beautiful. All separate islands? Really? Take away the water or go diving and what do you see? You see a continuous landscape with hills and valleys, all connected, all one.

The separate islands are revealed to be an illusion brought on by their true reality being obscured by the water.

Well what if we are like those islands, our separateness being an illusion brought on by our inability to perceive ourselves as one continuous energy field?

That's about as far as most people take this idea but not me. I'm even more weird.

About ten years ago I was stopping over in Santander waiting to catch a ferry to Portsmouth so I wandered off to explore the town. It was packed, crowded, busy as hell. Suddenly, while forcing my way through the crowds, I was struck by a very strange idea. Whether an inspiration, insight, enlightenment or sheer madness is for you to decide.

I suddenly realised that all these people were actually, literally me. I had always believed in reincarnation. Since I was a very small child I just understood it and couldn't understand why everyone didn't know it. Nobody had told be about it, I hadn't heard it anywhere, I was too small. I just knew.

But as I grew up I starting reading about it and just fell in with the general consensus that we are all separate, reincarnating souls. This Santander revaluation was something quite different.

I had long understood that time is not linear. Indeed time does not really exist at all in the way we usually think of it. Incarnations don't occur one after the other in a straight line, there is no past or future, its all happening right now, in this moment. All your, mine, their past, future and concurrent incarnations, all happening right now in this moment. And not just people but every life form in the universe.

So, if you can accept that, its not a huge leap to accept that we are all just different incarnations of the same soul, different expressions of THE ONE, the one soul, Source, God, or whatever term you like to use.

Call it what you will, I call it Universal Love. We are a part of Universal Love just as Universal Love is a part of us. We can never be separated from Universal Love except in so far as our belief in that separation makes it so for us.

We are all God pretending to be you and me and him and her. We are The Universe experiencing itself.

I certainly don't want to offend anyone's religious sensibilities here. You don't need to agree with me on this in order to understand and enjoy the rest of this book. But if you do want to run with this it will certainly help you to never harm anyone. If the person in your face, really is you experiencing another incarnation, how can you hate or want to harm yourself?

So when I encourage you all to be excellent to each-other I am really asking you to be excellent to all the different versions of you.

If someone is behaving badly it is only because they don't yet understand what you understand. What is annoying you is really another version of you who does not yet know the things you have learnt. Or maybe just a reflexion of something you need to work on in your present incarnation. So don't fight him or her. Help that other version of you to reach the understanding you have reached.

You may well see things other people, other versions of you, don't see yet. Be kind to them anyway, You may well see things that I don't see yet. Be kind to me anyway,

Moving on ....

I have put together a blueprint for a happier, more peaceful, more loving futuristic world. A common sense blueprint of love and tolerance that is neither left wing nor right wing but that draws wisdom form many sources.

I am certainly not advocating appeasement but rather to work towards helping *others* to understand what we understand. Don't hate the wrongdoers even if you do hate what they are doing. We really don't need to hate anyone, no mater how badly they are behaving. Rather let's help them to see that it can be a better way.

There will be nothing easy about it. It will be a long, uphill struggle to reach that futuristic world, that true UTOPIA, but one very much worth undertaking, one day at a time, one act of kindness at a time, one act of defiance at a time.

Utopia? I talk a lot about that. Some of you have told me that you don't like the word because it has been misused in the past. Well this book is about the future not the past. Every time you read *utopia* in this book please forget the past and try to visualise a better world, the world I described earlier in this chapter. We really can get there if we all pull together.

Its probably too late for us but we can build a better world for our grandchildren and great-grandchildren, if we start now, by adopting these principles and values and by teaching them to our children, in the home, at school, and in our churches, synagogues, mosques and temples.

We can only get there, one day, if we begin to navigate in that direction today. Who is with me? If you share my dream please do share this free book widely. I would also very much appreciate your feedback. I can be contacted via this book's website website https://lovenotfear.uk

So please do help spread the word and share this book. The world is going through a very challenging time. Governments around the world are becoming ever more tyrannical. People everywhere are looking for answers.

How can we find our way out of this mess?

My response to that is, don't follow me or anyone else. Just open your heart to unconditional love and do what you feel to be right. Open your heart. Not you head, your head is connected to your very limited five senses perception of reality. It is full of doubts and fears. Your heart, on the other hand, can sense all of reality, if you let it, and unconditional love knows no fear. Breathe deeply and relax, open up your heart, and you will know what action to take.

The rest of this book will give you plenty of suggestions but never let any book replace your own heart felt truths. We are many and they are few. Together we can build a better, freer world, one act of kindness at a time, one act of defiance at a time.

Namaste.

CHAPTER TWO - Be excellent to each-other and to the environment

"Even while we pray to God to save us, the power to save ourselves is in our own hands. If we just stop doing things that hurt each other, the Earth would quickly resemble Heaven."

Alan Cohen

This is what I like to call The First Pillar of Utopia. It is the main, fundamental principle. The other pillars, as I call them, are really just some of the ways we can implement this first fundamental principle. This does not necessarily mean loving your enemy or tolerating abuse. It does not mean allowing yourself to become a victim. Not everyone will be on the same path to utopia that we are on. This principle is about being excellent to others on the same path, or on a neutral path, to animals and to our Mother Earth, but not to those who want to hurt us and do us harm. By all means send them love, hold them in the light, but it's also important to protect ourselves and our loved ones and to stay safe.

Treat everyone with love, while staying safe. We are all doing the best we can in every moment. Some peoples' best may seem pretty awful to us but it's not our place to judge others. We can judge and condemn what they do but not the people themselves. Had they had more resourceful upbringings, in loving homes, in peaceful regions of the world, where resources were fairly shared, been taught more resourceful, kind and tolerant values, been taught to respect other countries, other cultures and other religions, their actions now would be much more noble.

Nobody is past redemption, so never give up on anyone. Everyone can learn more resourceful ways to behave. It is my dearest hope that this little book will play a part in inspiring people everywhere to treat each-other fairly, indeed to be excellent to each-other and spread the love.

Many years ago I watched a rather silly teenage movie called Bill and Ted's Excellent Adventure. It was fun but hardly thought provoking. Nevertheless something about it stuck in my mind. Rather than saying something like "have a nice day", Bill and Ted would declare, with high fives, *be excellent to each-other*.

That got me thinking, if only we could all just be excellent to each-other and to the environment, we would be living in paradise, we would have utopia.

We live on a beautiful planet which gives us more than enough resources for everybody to live in comfort. We would all live in paradise if we could just stop being rotten to each-other.

It must start with each one of us as individuals. So let's

make a start, right now, and begin turning this nightmare world into a loving utopia.

Be excellent to each-other. Be fair to each-other. Treat everyone as an equal, regardless of race, religion or gender. Change our focus away from *how much can I get* and instead think *how much can I give.*

Not any time soon I hear you say. Yes absolutely, I accept it will take time; time and persistence, but we will get there if we believe we can and if we want it badly enough. I really do believe that.

The question then arises *how can we be excellent to those who are treating us badly?*

I don't have any easy answer to this. Some of us believe in turning the other cheek. Others are into revenge. Revenge is understandable enough but is ultimately an unresourceful strategy. As Gandhi famously said *An eye for and eye will make the whole world blind*

Most of us probably take a more pragmatic position somewhere in between.

A popular saying at the moment is *that which we feed energy to expands, that which we deny energy to contracts.* I believe there is a lot of truth in tins, within limits.

If you are being chased by a leopard, sitting on the ground visualising an empty space where the predator is

16

probably won't save your life. Maybe one day, when we are all a lot more spirituality advanced but not yet. Better to get out of there fast and be more vigilant in the future. Watch your back. Watch four friends' backs. Don't be a victim.

Meerkats post a sentry. If an eagle or a snake approaches they give a warning. The other meerkats don't accuse the sentry of spreading hatred towards eagles and snakes. We need to be like those meerkats and warn each-other of potential dangers from those who are not yet ready to embrace our utopian, egalitarian philosophy.

Don't spread hate, spread awareness, and never accuse those spreading awareness of spreading hate. Well meaning organisations such as *Hope Not Hate* wind up spreading far more hate than hope, unfortunately.

Its important that we keep this as a grass roots movement. We need to be able to think clearly and see clearly, free from the influences of so-called *political correctness*, political parties, biased media or our corrupted educational system which is designed to turn out passive, compliant workers rather than free thinkers.

Challenge every belief. Ask *do I really believe this or did I just learn it at school or at university?* Just because everyone else you know believes something doesn't necessarily make it true. Do your own research and draw your own conclusion. Be a free-thinker.

Just because it's in the papers doesn't necessarily mean

it's true. I wrote a book recently about how media barons, central banks, arms dealers and politicians conspire together to weave a web of lies to keep us under control. It's called *Rupert Murdoch's Hitmen* if you want to check it out. It's on Amazon.

We need to see each separate issue for what it really is, irrespective of some party dogma. Political parties, left, right or centre, are not what they pretend to be. If you support any particular party you are expected to buy into their whole manifesto, the bits you agree with as well as the stuff that makes no sense at all.

You don't have to believe everything I say and I don't expect you will. Your idea of utopia will be different from mine in some respects. Even when we have a million supporters, we will still have a million slightly different definitions of utopia. That's healthy. We are individual people not clones.

Here is a poem I rather like by Grenville Kleiser (1868 - 1935)

If I can do some good today,
If I can serve along life's way,
If I can something helpful say,
Lord show me how.

If I can right a human wrong,
If I can help to make one strong,

If I can cheer with smile or song,
Lord show me how.

If I can make a burden less,
If I can aid one in distress,
If I can spread more happiness,
Lord show me how.

If I can do a kindly deed,
If I can show a fruitful seed,
If I can help someone in need,
Lord show me how.

If I can feed a hungry heart,
If I can give a better start,
If I can fill a nobler part,
Lord show me how.

If you feel in need of daily inspiration I highly recommend The Inspirational Blog. FREE: Inspiring quotes and videos from Rumi, Douglas Adams, Richard Bach, Buddha, Keanu Reeves, Sir Winston Churchill, Alan Cohen, Gangaji, Robert Holden, A Course in Miracles and many more to lift your spirits. https://the-inspirational-blog.org/

The world will not be saved by politicians but by the small deeds of each and every one of us. Every time we choose, you and I, to be excellent to somebody or to the environment, we are moving society TOWARDS UTOPIA.

CHAPTER THREE - Generosity

We are trying to build a world where people earn respect and status according to what they put into society, instead of what they take out for themselves. The focus has to be on how much we can give, not how much we can get.

Money Is The Root Of All Meanness

Money is a more sophisticated form of barter. At least that's what we are told.

Barter is often summed up as *I'll give you this if you give me that.*

It could be better summed up as *I will ONLY give you this if you give me that.*

Is it really human nature to be so mean or have we been conned somewhere along the way? Have we been instilled with a fake and unfounded fear, a fear that enables the Globalist Elite to control us?

What would happen if we tried something different? *I'll give you this because I have two and you have none and you look like you could use one.*

That would bring down the whole corrupt system. It would cause a revolution. We need a peaceful revolution to destroy the power of the Globalist Elite so let's give it go.

This is not communism or socialism. Far be it for me to support communism. I consider communism to be an evil system. Having said that I love the communist manifesto *For each according to his ability, to each according to his need.* That's beautiful. It's simply another way of saying that we are all our brother's keeper. It's just the communist implementation of this beautiful idea which is ugly. It all goes wrong when that beautiful seed idea is administered by government.

Politics is corrupting and all governments, by their very nature, become corrupt. But if we lived in an informal gift economy, with no money and nobody keeping score, with everybody doing what they could for each other and taking what was offered by others according to their need, we would live in paradise. It's only when governments get involved that the whole thing goes tits up. Communism is supposed to be about the people holding all the wealth collectively but what it really is, is the government holding all the wealth and turning the people into slaves.

What I am talking about is people owning their own wealth but being generous with it. This puts the people in control, each and every one of us individually. It's

22

about us all taking care of each other without interference from any government or welfare state.

And the beauty is that we don't need anyone's permission to do it. We can start to live that way today just by deciding to do it. If we do then the Globalist Elite are screwed.

There is more than enough wealth for every one of us but we are separated from it by fear. And our fear makes us mean to others which gives them good reason to be fearful. Then their fear makes them mean which makes others fearful and mean. And around and around we go on the everlasting, ever perpetuating carousel of fear until someone shouts STOP !!!

Well I am shouting STOP right now. That's why I wrote this book. We don't have to go on living like this. There is a better way.

The Rise Of The Robots

Tired of the 9 to 5 grind? Fed up with working your arse off just to make a rich man or woman even richer? Relax. Chances are that problem won't be bothering you much longer.

Your job will soon be taken by a robot. Robotics are playing an increasing role in manufacturing industry as well as other sectors but who will benefit?

Lets begin by looking briefly at basic economics. Karl Marx wrote a lot of daft things but he did make some sensible observations too. He wrote about power and wealth belong to the owners of the means of production.

Early in the Industrial Revolution this meant that the rich factory owners held all the cards and could create a society that served their needs. They would share as little wealth as they could get away with, with the workers, keeping them in perpetual poverty. This is the classic capitalist model.

The leaders of the Russian Revolution promised to overturn capitalism by bringing the ownership of the means of production into the hands of the people. Great idea, except that was not what they did. Instead they put the ownership of the means of production into the hands of the government. They created a centrally planned, communist society. The people had simply exchanged one oppressor for another.

Communism has pretty much failed everywhere its been tried and the watered down versions of socialism that do survive are struggling. Coming up to the more technological societies we have today, highly qualified and specialised workers can demand higher wages but unless they own the means of production they are still playing the rich man's game. Over the next fifty years or so robots will be taking more and more people's jobs. Workers will lose out while those who own the robots will do very well for themselves.

There is a growing cry from the political left to give socialism another go, to over-tax the rich and provide welfare benefits to the unemployed masses keeping them as vessels of the state.

Even more sinister is Agenda 21/30 which seeks to kill off the vessels of the state, billions of them. Agenda 21/30 is an action plan of the United Nations with regard to sustainable development. It is a product of the Earth Summit held in Rio de Janei-ro, Brazil, in 1992. Some of its wider and more sinister implications include depopulating vast areas of the globe.

Let's face facts, our planet is seriously over populated. We desperately do need to reduce our numbers, urgently. But do we really need to be culled? Are we really so stupid that we can't control our own urge to reproduce?

The problem with both communist and capitalist economic systems is that as the birth rate drops, we end up with an unsustainable transition period were there are insufficient working age people to support a disproportionate number of pensioners.

But there is a better way, not communism, not socialism, not capitalism but a totally new approach to the problem. We can, if we chose, build a totally free, democratic society with small, light handed governments that obey the people.

Robots will soon take many of our jobs but there is a

positive side too. Robots will do most of the work freeing their owners to enjoy more leisure time. Their owners will be able to programme their robots to make them whatever they need. Who will those lucky owners be? That's the big question. Will they be the same people who own the factories now? Or will they be some domineering, totalitarian government of the future?

Or will we choose today to start to build a more egalitarian future? A society where the robots serve the people, not the governments and not the capitalists but every single one of us. A future without money or barter where we all freely give and freely receive.

But what about human nature? What about the cheaters? Richard Dawkins, author of The Selfish Gene, wrote about the *cheaters* and the *suckers*. Won't they run amok in a free society?

I admit it's a risk but I also believe that thieves and con-artists are motivated by fear, the fear of not having enough of life's riches and the fear of not being good enough to make an honest living. Some, of course, are just afraid of hard work.

In a society where everything is free for the taking and most of the hard graft is done my autonomous machines, what remains to motivate the cheaters? Not much. The truth is that there is more than enough wealth to go around. Poverty, lack and austerity are artificial constructs designed to keep us in debt slavery. It's all a conspiracy by the globalist elite. It's not real.

So let's get rid of money, banksters and accountants and start to enjoy the bounty this planet has to offer. It's our birth right after all. Right now, as I write this updated paragraph in March 2020, we are being urged to stop using cash in case it spreads disease. They want us to use plastic money instead so they can keep tabs on everything we earn and everything we spend. What a con! So instead of just giving up cash, let's give up money altogether. That'll fuk 'em.

The great thing about this new idea is that we don't need to lobby the government to make it happen. We can begin small today and watch it grow. We can begin today just by treating people better, being generous to each other, being excellent to each other. The more we can freely give and freely receive among each other, and the more we can avoid using money and the banks, the more power we can wrestle out of the hands of the globalist elite and the governments they control.

When we still do need to buy stuff, let's make sure, as far as possible, that it's locally produced. Little by little we can do this, we can win. We will win!

The Globalist Elite

I talk a lot about the Globalist Elite and the Deep State in my books but who exactly are they?

You probably already know of them by another name such as *the Cabal* or *the Illuminati*. Some say they are just an informal bunch of high ranking Freemasons. Whatever you call them, we are talking about the people who attend Bilderberg Group conferences and Bohemian Grove rituals.

There have been many different, interconnected secret societies throughout recorded history and even earlier. The term *the Illuminati* really is just a shorthand, collective term for all these different people. It is said that their ultimate goal is world domination by inflicting a totalitarian world government upon us. I believe this is true.

Governments in Britain, Europe, America and other places have done too many stupid things to be credible. Two world wars, not to mention the invasion of Iraq which directly caused the formation of Isis as well as fuelling the refugee crisis that is now destabilising the western world. This has been a deliberately engineered crisis to further the globalist agenda.

We would have to be completely blind not to see a pattern unfolding. Especially so when we consider the mounting evidence that the so-called 9/11 assault on the Twin Towers in New York may well have been a false flag attack.

The globalist elite take our freedoms by inflicting fear and then offering fake solutions that rob us of our power. They are behind both sides of all wars. They are behind mass immigration and terrorism. And they were behind the Great Depression and all subsequent recessions.

David Icke has done a very thorough job tracing their bloodlines all the way back to ancient Babylon and Sumer. If you are interested I strongly recommend his book *The Truth Shall Make You Free* and others. David Icke is a brilliant writer, speaker and researcher but sometimes, in my own humble opinion, he goes a bit too far. He gets some things wrong sometimes, as do I, as do we all. Please don't let this distract you from the core truths unearthed by his excellent research. You don't need to believe everything he says, and I most certainly don't, in order to benefit from his research into the Globalist Elite families and the control they wield in the world.

You might also like to check out writers such as Edwin Black and Jim Marrs. I particularly recommend Edwin Black's books, especially *The Farhud*, if you are interested in the connections between the Arabs and Nazi Germany. I am not telling you what to believe, I am not too sure myself, I am just pointing you to three rather different viewpoints so you can decide for yourself. Whatever the details, something very fishy is definitely afoot.

I believe that nearly all presidents and prime ministers have been members of Globalist Elite families, as have the captains of industry, bankers and media barons and royal families. They control everything. Again please refer to Icke, Black and Marrs, and my book *Rupert*

Murdoch's Hitmen for full details.

The more you study and research these things the more hopeless it seems. The Globalist Elite control everything, our banking system, our education system, our industry, our entertainment industry, our military, our political system. Everyone is playing their game, singing their tune, we are all being played and controlled.

It would be so easy to just give up hope and surrender to their globalist agenda. But before you decide to throw in towel please consider this. They are few and we are many. If we all stand up, united, shoulder to shoulder and just refuse to comply they lose and we win. We just have to say *NO MORE, we didn't devise this game and we are not playing it any longer.*

Ironically that great illuminati Grand Master and founder of the Jesuit movement, Saint Ignatius of Loyola (1491 - 1556), gave us the key to defeating the globalist elite. His famous prayer begins with the following words *"Teach us, good Lord, to serve you as you deserve, to give and not to count the cost, ... to toil and not to seek for rest, to labour and not to ask for any reward."*

Clearly he meant for us to give to the Illuminati, in its guise as the Christian church, without any reward but if we take his words literally we really can beat the globalist elite. (I am not attacking Christians here. I have great respect for genuinely religious people of all faiths. I refer only to the self-serving elite who have infiltrated these groups and turned then into authoritarian institutions).

The illuminati own the world's banking system. It's their main tool of control. They lend us money they don't have and charge us interest on it. What kind of sick mind could devise a scam such as credit? They lend us money that doesn't really exist (banks can lend ten times more than they have in reserve, and it's legal) to buy a house and when we can't make our repayments on time they steal the house and make us homeless. That can't possibly be right.

By keeping us in debt, and in fear of defaulting on the debt, they turn us into slaves. The globalist elite use debt to keep us in slavery so let's stop borrowing money for a start. Then, in a few years time, let's go the whole hog and stop using money altogether. That will upset 'em!

Let's give to each-other and not count the cost. Let's toil for each-other and not ask for any reward.

We won't need any reward because everyone else will be giving to us and toiling for us freely and generosity too. We just need to stop competing among ourselves and start co-operating. Stop fighting each-other over who has the best religion or who should be in charge and just start being excellent to each-other.

Light and Darkness - Some people like to think in terms of the forces of light battling the forces of darkness.

31

While it's important not to associate these forces with any particular religion or political group the idea can be a useful one. We can think of the good, loving, generous, broad-minded, tolerant people of the world, the forces of light, in a struggle with the globalist elite, the forces of darkness. We don't do battle with guns and bombs of course. We are here to spread our love and light, not to spread hatred.

Beware however that one of the tactics used by the globalist elite is to accuse those critical of their plans of so-called *hate speech*. It ain't necessarily so. Before you can shine your light into the darkness you need to know where the darkness is. How can pointing that out to folk possibly be *hate speech*? Well I shine my light into many dark corners in this book.

We can only defeat the forces of darkness with love and light. We can spread our love and light daily through acts of kindness. We can also raise our vibration through meditation. I like to begin and end each day with a love and light meditation where I focus on becoming a beacon of love and light.

The time has come to set ourselves free from the globalist elite. Who's with me?

Money and Wealth

Maybe success in life is less about making money and more about developing ourselves into people who are of value to others. Maybe its less about acquiring wealth and more about building a better world for all humankind.

Of course there is nothing wrong with wealth. The more we have the more we can help others and share. What's more, there is plenty for everyone, or at least there will be when selfish people stop hoarding it. Wealth is energy and energy needs to be allowed to flow freely. So let's help each-other to have enough, that's what being excellent to each-other really means. Nobody ever needs to live in poverty and it's up to every single one of us to ensure that nobody ever does live in poverty.

But money? That's a different thing entirely. Why do we need Money? What is it good for? Only one thing. Money enables us to keep score. It lets us tell who is winning and who is losing. That's it. Apart from that it does far more harm than good in the world.

Imagine if you will, some future world where people no longer care who is winning and who is losing. Imagine if you will, some future world were people gain status by putting more into society, rather than by taking more out for themselves (big house, fast car). Imagine if you will, some future world were people are generous, where they think "how much can I give" rather than "how much can I get". Imagine if you will, some future world were people live by the motto "Be excellent to each-other".

Such a world would have no need for money or barter. Everyone would make stuff or provide a service, to give away, freely, never counting the cost, in the knowledge that whatever goods and services they need will be given freely to them by other people.

I am not talking about a centrally planned economy here. I am not talking about some heavy handed, interfering government. People would be naturally incentivised to provide goods and services that are in demand because that's how status and respect are earned. Useless, vanity projects would earn zero respect or status.

All the jobs that are being done now will still need to be done, with the exception of banking, accountancy and finance. We will have no need for insurance either because when unforeseen events occur, everyone will rally round and help. Help will come first from local people but where a disaster hits a whole region or country, help will come flooding in from far and wide, everyone being excellent to each-other. That's the first and most important pillar of utopia - Be excellent to each-other.

Factory jobs will still exist. Stuff still needs to be manufactured, Some people are happiest when working with their hands, others prefer office work. There will be no difference in the status of these different jobs, why would there be? This is something we can start now, at school, teaching that manual work is just as important as white collar work.

Company politics will follow the first pillar of utopia - Be excellent to each-other. Managers will probably be called coordinators, it will be their job to ensure the company is manufacturing the things people actually want or need and to liaise with suppliers of parts and raw materials.

The world is not ready for such a system yet, too many people are too shallow and too greedy for such a system to work. The time will come, just not yet. First we have to work at removing the fear from peoples' lives and that's what the rest of this book is about.

But some people are ready for it now. There are Streetbank and Freecycle groups all over Britain and similar things in other countries. Type *free economy* into your favourite search engine and see what comes up.

These groups tend to be used to give away things people have bought and no longer need. The next step could be for people to make or grow stuff specifically to give away on these groups. Perhaps people could get together to run local free economies, like hippy communes only on a larger scale. My dream is to try out such a community on an island somewhere. One day. Anyone here got an island we can use?

If you want to explore these ideas further I highly recommend two books by *Mark Boyle*, *The Moneyless Man* and *The Moneyless Manifesto*.

Just because I want a money free world one day please

don't think I am against wealth. Wealth is fantastic and I want each and every one of us to have a whole lot more of it to use for good. Most success coaches will tell you that money is an energy that allows you to be all that you can be. I say that wealth is an energy that allows you to be all that you can be. Money is just a token of exchange, a way to quantify wealth, a way of telling who is winning and losing at the wealth game.

Do you see the difference? In the futuristic Utopia I think we can one day attain, we won't care who is winning and who is losing. Indeed the focus will be outward, not inward. The motive of all generous, tolerant, broad-minded, loving people will be to maximise the wealth of their generous, tolerant, broad-minded, loving neighbours.

Of course we can't just turn off all the money computers today. There would be chaos. The people who hate their jobs, and that's a lot of people, would simply not turn up for work. Shops would be empty and people would starve. We need to be a bit more cleaver than that. We need to start slowly and build up to it over several years. I am writing the first draft of this chapter in 2017. I propose Winter Solstice 2075 as Utopia Day. That will give us ten years to get this little book into the hands of millions of people worldwide, especially the decision makers, captains of industry, school teachers and university lectures. We really need to begin teaching our youngsters these principles right away.

Then we have a further 48 years for the kids starting

36

school in ten years time to grow up and have kids of their own and for those kids to grow up. It also gives us time for all the boring, unpleasant jobs to be taken over by machines.

We don't live in that world yet but for reasons I explain in this book, I still want us to focus on helping other generous, tolerant, broad-minded, loving people before ourselves. Apart from the moral imperative, its easier to create wealth when you want to use it to help others. So let's not scare money away now by thinking it's bad. It isn't the money that's bad at all. Its the greed and selfishness that are bad. In fact having money in today's world is extremely empowering so long as we use it for good.

So letâ€™s take a look at some of the other things we can do to remove the fear from our lives and replace it with love.

CHAPTER FOUR - Tolerance and respect for all other broad-minded, tolerant people

This absolutely does not mean walking around on eggshells trying not to offend intolerant, small-minded fools. Tolerant people are not easily offended and intolerant people don't share our vision of utopia.

We can only build our better world, our utopia, with tolerance and respect for all other broad-minded, tolerant people. Indeed Utopia requires that all people, everywhere, be loving, broad-minded and tolerant. That's the only way this utopia thing is going to work. We are all different and its our differences that make us so very special.

We all have different ideas on how to live a good life. We all like doing different things, we have different things we are good at, different hobbies, and different ways we express our creativity. And we each have our own different, unique ways of contributing to society.

Its no coincidence that I used the word 'different' al lot there. We are all different in a multitude of beautiful ways. Life would be so boring were we all the same. It is the variety of individual expression that makes life interesting.

The central tenet of the Towards Utopia Movement is *Be Excellent to Each-other* so we should encourage each-other's individuality and try to help each-other express that individuality.

Of course if the way you like to express your individuality is, for instance, to play your music really loudly, and you live in a close proximity to other people with different musical tastes, you are not really being excellent to them, are you now? Be excellent to your neighbours and get some headphones! Either that or move away.

Where tolerance tends to go wrong is when we are told we have to tolerate the intolerable. It's important that we don't use tolerance to excuse bad behaviour. In this nightmare world we have built for ourselves we are told it's not *politicly correct* to criticise certain people or groups. I'm sorry but to me this is totally intolerable, this is fascism, this is totalitarianism, and its on the rise in the western world.

Intolerance is the failure to appreciate and respect the practices, opinions and beliefs of other groups but that isn't always a bad thing. When another group is acting illegally or against the best interests of the majority, its our duty to speak out. For example the systematic rape and torture of some 1,400 young girls in Rotherham, in the north of England. These atrocities were carried on between 1997 and 2013 by organised gangs of predominantly Pakistani Muslim men. The police and local government officials knew it was going on but took no action in the interests of so-called *social cohesion*. Since all this came to light it's been discovered that similar gangs operated all over Britain and had been ignored everywhere. This is a clear example of taking tolerance way too far.

In our enthusiasm for tolerance, we have actually become a deeply intolerant society. We pass legislation to police so-called *hate speech*, we abuse climate change sceptics, and neo-atheists lambast religious believers. The liberal dream has clearly gone wrong. Many of the people who pride themselves on being liberal are quite clearly no longer liberal at all.

There is a very interesting book by sociologist Frank Furedi that I would refer you to. It's called *On Tolerance: A Defence of Moral Independence*

The problem is that tolerance, in its classical liberal sense as a virtue essential to freedom, has been hijacked and bankrupted. Dragged into the politicisation of identity, tolerance has become a form of "polite etiquette". Where once it was about the tolerance of individuals and their opinions, it has now been redeployed to deal with group conflicts. Once it was about opening the mind to competing beliefs, now it is about one that affirms different groups. Along this slippery path, much of the original importance of tolerance has been distorted or lost.

We are now being told it's a so-called *hate crime* if some intolerant person we are criticising for his or her intolerance, takes *offence* at our criticism. How ridiculous is this? What a crazy, backwards world we do live in.

We must always protect our free speech and that includes the right to criticise wrongdoing as well as any political ideas we happen to disagree with. Without free and open debate on all subjects, democracy becomes impotent, a mere sham. Our new, better world needs to be rooted in true, power to the people, grass roots democracy and we can't have that without free speech.

The thing about free speech is that to work at all, it has to apply equally to those we agree with and to those we vehemently disagree with and that, my friends, is the true meaning of tolerance.

As William Ury wrote in *Getting To Peace*, "tolerance is not just agreeing with one another or remaining indifferent in the face of injustice, but rather showing respect for the essential humanity in every person."

We don't have to agree with each other in order to respect each other and just because we disagree certainly doesn't mean we hate each other. Tolerance and respect only work when they are reciprocated. This is a big problem with a small minority of newcomers we welcome into out tolerant land. Instead of asking stupid questions about pop groups and long dead statesmen in our citizenship tests, we need to ask deep probing questions concerning their attitudes to free speech, equality, freedom of religion, tolerance and respect.

Population

This of course leads into another important pillar of Utopia, maintain a stable population. One of the problems we have today is there are just too many of us. Too many people crammed into too small a space. This, coupled with poverty, leads to overcrowded conditions where we have far more opportunities to annoy one and other.

So let's limit our population so we all have plenty of room in which to express ourselves without interfering with others.

Which brings me neatly back to respect, respect for our planet and all her natural systems, taking only what we need. Mother Earth gives us life. Without her benevolence we would die. We must love and revere her, worship her as a goddess as our ancestors had the good sense to do. Buy organic, locally sourced food or grow your own. Walk or cycle to work, invest in local, small-scale renewable energy, use local butchers, grocers, green grocers and fish mongers rather than the big supermarkets.

Utopia will be a network of co-operating, small-scale, decentralised, self-sufficient communities NOT some impersonal, totalitarian, globalised mega-state. By looking after our home planet and the other people and creatures we share it with, we will always have a truly utopian place in which to live and express ourselves.

World Peace

Can you imagine a world without war? We've been led to believe that war is normal, a part of being human. Well, it's not.

And political suppression isn't normal either, nor is poverty. There's enough food to feed the entire world. The problem is uneven distribution of the Earth's resources because of greed. And greed is caused by fear.

Taxes are not normal, indeed money itself is not normal. Money is just a way of keeping score, of knowing who is winning and who is losing in the game of greed and meanness.

Can you even begin to understand how generous we could all be if we weren't living in fear, if we knew all our needs would be met and nobody was out to get us? Can you even begin to imagine what fair distribution of wealth would be like if we lived in Love Not Fear? Not distributed by governments but by peer to peer generosity, among free, independent people freed from fear.

If we all respected each other and each other's national borders we could live in peace. It's the responsibility of every single one of us to make it happen. Tolerant, generous, respectful people would have nothing to fight and kill for, there would be no need to cheat or steal, nothing to get hung up about.

Let me share a powerful quotation from Conversations With God by Neale Donald Walsch:

Bring peace to the earth by bringing peace to all those whose lives you touch.

Be peace.

Feel and express in every moment, your divine connection with The All and with every person, place, and thing.

Embrace every circumstance, own every fault, share every joy, contemplate every mystery, walk in every man's shoes, forgive every offence, including your own, heel every heart, honour every person's truth, adore every person's god, protect every person's rights, preserve every person's dignity, promote every person's interests, provide every person's needs, presume every person's holiness, present every person's greatest gifts, produce every person's blessing and pronounce every person's future secure in the assured love of God.

Be a living, breathing example of the highest truth that resides within you.

Speak humbly of yourself, lest some mistake your highest truth for a boast.

Speak softly, lest someone think you are merely calling for attention.

Speak gently, that all might know of love.

Speak openly, lest anyone think you have something to hide.

Speak candidly, so you cannot be mistaken.

Speak often so that your word may today go forth.

Speak, respectfully, that no one be dishonoured.

Speak lovingly, that every syllable may heal.

Make your life a gift.

Remember, always. You are a gift.

CHAPTER FIVE - Respect our planet and all her natural systems

Let's take only what we need. Mother Earth gives us life. Without her benevolence we would die. We must love and revere her, worship her as a goddess as our ancestors had the good sense to do.

An essential part of being able to live with love and not fear is being confident that some prat somewhere isn't messing up the natural world that we all depend upon for our survival. We need to have faith that the air we breath is clean, the water we drink is wholesome and the food we eat hasn't been poisoned by agrochemicals. We need to know that our oceans aren't clogged with plastic and that there are enough trees to produce all the oxygen we need. In short we need to have confidence that all of the natural systems are working perfectly. A good place to start with the task of ending pollution is not to be that polluter.

To live in Utopia we will need to inhabit an utopian environment. Right now, that would seem to be a bit of a tall order. We have been systemically abusing Mother Earth since at least the start of the industrial revolution. It's time to turn the page and secure the critical benefits that nature provides to humanity, such as nutritious food, fresh water, clean air, and the huge wealth of other species who share this planet with us and enrich our lives.

And its not just other species. Many of the earth's threatened wildernesses are the traditional homelands of indigenous peoples. Native peoples living in these areas directly depend on the products of healthy ecosystems, harvesting wild plants and animals for their food, fuel, clothing, medicine and shelter. In nearly every case it is these native people who know best how to manage their own environments. We saw what happened in the recent brushfires in Australia when the aboriginal forest management systems had been abandoned in favour of modern methods.

The ancient knowledge of these societies is encoded in their economies as well as their, spiritual and cultural values and identities. They are deeply committed to maintaining the biodiversity of the ecosystems they depend upon. However, multiple pressures exerted on indigenous and other rural communities have made this a challenging proposition in many places. We must respect native peoples everywhere and protect them from arrogant, and often ignorant, newcomers.

Traditional Pagan and shamanistic societies knew how to look after the Earth and understood that people are an integral part of our home planet. They used the word *god* or *gods* to refer to natural processes like sun, moon, wind, storm and fertility. To them God was the soul of the universe just as the universe is the body of God. There was no separation, all were one. Earth was our mother and our goddess.

Then came along the Abrahamic religions with their teaching that God had given us dominion over the beasts of the field and the fish of the sea. Suddenly we suffered the illusion of being in charge, separate and aloof.

Fortunately we didn't have the technology to do too much damage for a very long time. Then came the industrial revolution and it was all down hill from there for our environment.

Its true that some religious teachers preached that there is a sacred trust between humankind and God under which we accept a duty of stewardship for the Earth but that message fell on deaf ears more often than not where there was money to be made.

More often, in recent decades at least, humanists and atheists have taken up the conservation cause on moral and ethical grounds. Add to them the groundswell of people joining the Pagan revival movement and we have, at long last, a formidable opposition to those eager to trash our planet for profit.

Of course we don't have to return to mud huts to save the environment. We can and should continue to progress technologically and scientifically. That is our destiny but we must strive for a genuinely sustainable form of development. In order to achieve that our industrialists and scientists will have to rediscover a sense of the sacred in our dealings with the natural world. They will have to remember that She is our mother and our goddess.

An understanding of the sacredness of Mother Earth will help us stay in balance and harmony with the rest of the natural world . It will enable us to set limits on our ambitions and set parameters for sustainable development.

In some cases nature's limits are well understood at the rational, scientific level. For example, we know that trying to graze too many goats on a hillside will prevent the regeneration of vegetation and in arid conditions can lead to desertification. We understand that the overuse of insecticides or antibiotics leads to problems of resistance and we are slowly beginning to wake up to the full, awful consequences of pumping too much industrial waste into our atmosphere and plastic and toxins into our oceans. And we are on the verge of discovering the consequences of allowing GMO crops to cross-pollinate with traditional cultivars.

Scientists tend to side with the environmentalists on these issues but their voices are small while those of multinational corporation are loud. Oil companies, agribusiness giants and Monsanto and the Rothschild run central banks that finance them are like an express train without brakes. They are perfectly willing and able to commission their own research anyway, thus ensuring they get the findings that they want.

Even when there is overwhelming public opposition to

an environmentally damaging project, such as with fracking for example, governments more often than not will side with the money, not the people.

It often seems that when we do have scientific evidence that we are damaging our environment we still aren't willing to do enough to put things right.

Public decision makers will often take back handers from the greedy, globalist corporations to nod proposals through. Where that is too controversial they will sit on their hands and do nothing. Commissioning another study is an oft used technique to kick difficult issues into the long grass.

We must move away from the attitude that nature is just a system that can be engineered for our own convenience. She is a living being, *Gaia*, our mother, our goddess. She is far more than just a nuisance to be evaded, manipulated, and exploited by technology and human ingenuity.

We really do need to show more respect for the genius of our Mother Earth. Her processes and feedback loops have been rigorously tested and refined over millions of years. We can work with Her, in an attitude of love and respect, or we can work against her. Its our choice but I will tell you one thing. If we insist on working against her, SHE WILL WIN !

So let's not go there. Let's mend our ways. Let's build our Utopia. We will have to start small.

If you are not already doing so, please consider starting to grow your own organic food.

If you are not already doing so, please consider starting to walk or cycle to work.

If you are not already doing so, please consider reducing the amount of stuff you buy and use. Reuse and recycle whenever possible. Cut down on what you throw away. Try to conserve natural resources and landfill space. Please try to shop wisely. Buy less plastic and bring a reusable shopping bag. Buy locally produced food and goods whenever possible. Cut down on food miles and support your local community. As far as possible, support your own countries' manufacturers. Where you can, go even more local than that. Buy from your own county, city, town or village. If you really do need a car, buy one that was built in the same country you are living in. Same with televisions, white goods, and everything else you purchase. That's the only way to beat the globalists who want to destroy our home planet for their profit.

If you are not already doing so, please consider increasing your own level of education and help to educate others. It's important that we all understand the issues. But it's equally important to study and read from lots of different sources. Don't just take one source as gospel. Those people could have a hidden agenda. Just look at the way the well meaning but in my opinion, misguided, vegan lobby has tried to hijack the climate change debate.

If you are not already doing so, please consider volunteering for cleanups in your area. You can get involved in protecting your watershed too. Don't send chemicals into our waterways. Choose non-toxic chemicals in the home and office. Please consider trying to conserve water. The less water we use, the less runoff and contaminated wastewater that eventually end up in the ocean.

Plant a tree. Trees provide food and oxygen, they help save energy, and they clean the air. The world needs a trillion more trees. Please do your bit.

By looking after our home planet we will always have a truly utopian place to live.

CHAPTER SIX - Co-operation and good will

between free, independent nations and free, independent citizens everywhere.

And this will require a healthy respect for national boundaries.

This is probably the most controversial chapter of this book. Expect to have your preconceived ideas severely challenged. Most people associate with either a left-wing or right-wing view of the world (according to the conventional model of politics). The right likes to blame foreigners and immigrants for everything that goes wrong while the left tries to absolve them from all blame no matter how badly they behave. So whichever camp you have been brought up in, expect to have your mind broadened.

Without strong boarders we would soon end up with a totalitarian world government, run by the globalist elite to keep the rest of us compliant. Some of you don't believe that, I know from your feedback that you have been taught at school or university that boarders cause wars, and that scrapping all the borders is the way forward. If you think that then please consider this ....

Blaming a country for causing its own invasion on the grounds that if there were no borders they could have been overthrown without a war is like telling a woman that she wouldn't have been raped if she had opened her legs willingly. I am sure you agree that both attitudes are totally unacceptable.

Its like telling her that if she willingly opened her legs for all comers there would have been no need to rape her. I am sorry but this is an outrage. Women and men have a right to maintain their boundaries and so do nations. Indeed it is absolutely essential if they are to maintain their identity.

Right at the beginning of this chapter, before we go any further, so there is no misunderstanding, I want to make it plain that I want to live in a world with totally open borders. I want us all to be free to travel, settle and work anywhere in the world we choose, with no visa, no work permit, no passport, and without any government knowing or caring where we are - eventually.

Why eventually? Why not now? As I hope you will have noticed by now, the central theme of this book has been about being excellent to each other and making that possible by freeing people from fear. That includes the fear of bad, disrespectful, entitled migrants. So before we can enjoy the benefits of open boarders, we will all need to learn how to travel and settle in other peoples' countries respectfully, without scaring the crap out of the people who were already there. If you don't like the word 'countries' then substitute 'place'. Any place where there were already people living before you arrived.

All countries are different and its their differences that make them special. We have about 200 different independent nations on the planet, each with its own unique set of customs and laws. In order to preserve this richness and diversity we must respect the right of the people of each nation to run their own affairs as they choose. People who do not like the conditions in the country of their ancestors should have two choices, campaign for change or leave.

People who want to settle in a new country should generally be allowed to do so provided they love their new country just the way it is and don't try to make changes there. It is the responsibility of the newcomer to adapt and fit in with the established population, not the other way around. That's why multiculturalism is failing. Multi-ethnic is great but only when everyone embraces the same basic cultural values. We are blessed with 200 different, unique, beautiful countries so we can have 200 different, unique, beautiful cultures.

No government or supranational organisation has the right to interfere in the internal affairs of another country or to try and bring about regime change there. We must stop attacking and invading other peoples' countries. John Lennon was wrong when he asked us to imagine a world with no countries and no religion. People need countries and religions.

We need countries to give us a sense of belonging, something to be proud of. You are proud of your own achievements aren't you? And you are proud of the achievements of your children. So you are proud of your family. That's healthy.

On the next level up you may be proud of your town or your county. You may even cheer your town's football team or your county's cricket or baseball team on a Saturday afternoon. That's healthy too.

Up one more level and you are proud of your country and support your national football team in the World Cup. Or you may relate better to Wimbledon or to the Eurovision Song Contest. Whatever, its all positive and healthy. Never let anyone tell you different. I agree that it can become unhealthy when the traditional cultural values around sportsmanship are ignored, when athletes cheat or supporters fight each other in the streets. But that is not what I'm talking about here and it most certainly is not inevitable. When something goes wrong you don't scrap it, you fix it

So yes, problems can arise when people get abusive or violent, football hooliganism and wars and stuff. There's no need for all that. But we don't try to control football hooliganism by banning football do we? Of course not. We combat the real problem which is the hooliganism, we don't use football as a scapegoat. And we shouldn't use nationalism, or religion, as a scapegoat either. In this book I am using the word *nationalism* to mean the opposite of *globalism*, not to be confused with any supremacy movements and all that nonsense. People keep telling me I should refrain from using the word *nationalism* because of its negative associations. I prefer to dig a bit deeper. I prefer to ask why the word has negative associations? Where do those negative associations come from?

Academics define the word in negative ways. Of course they do. They are globalists. Accademia has been infiltrated by globalists for decades. Of course they want us to think bad things about nationalists and good things about globalists. They will tell you that Hitler called his party the *National Socialist German Workers' Party*. Of course the same academics who insist on the *nationalist* bit throw their dummies out of their prams when you mention the *socialist* bit.

So let's forget what we are told to believe and look at what the Nazis actually did. Did they respect other countries' sovereignty and borders as nationalist would do? No they invaded other countries and attempted to rule the world, just as globalists have always tried to do. So were they nationalists? Clearly they were not. They were globalists. *Nationalism* is a good word, let's reclaim it.

Be proud. Unfortunately some people misunderstand pride. They think that to be proud means you think yourself better than other people, or you think your country is better than other countries or your religion is better than other religions. This is absolutely not what I am talking about here. I am talking of a pride that makes you know, at a deep level, that you are the equal of everyone else. I am talking of a pride that makes you stand up straight and look other people in the eye. I am talking of a pride that gives you self-confidence.

Until we eventually reach that glorious, anarchist utopia of which I speak, we are going to need countries to ensure accountable democracy. We need national governments for the same reason we need borough councils and other levels of local government. They enable decisions to be made locally, by the people who will be affected by them. We really don't want to be dictated to by over-centralised levels of government. We are all different and one size most certainly does not fit all.

That is why the European Union is falling apart. All EU countries are unique and different and one size most certainly does not fit all. Had the EU stuck to its original mandate of being a free trade zone all would have been fine, but instead it became dictatorial, interfering in the rights of member countries to make their own laws. People just won't stand for that.

The EU is rapidly going the same way as the old USSR, and pretty much for the same reasons. The people of Europe still need to co-operate but it has to be co-operation between free, independent nations.

It will soon be time to establish the European Network of Free, Independent Nations (ENFIN). No political union, just free trade, friendship and co-operation.

Most of the wars since World War 2 have been caused by ethnic or religious groups that were sick and tiered of being forcefully enfolded into countries run by different ethnic or religious groups. Instead of being content to live in a relatively big country with people who have an incompatible culture or different political or religious needs, they rebel and try to form their own smaller, self governing country.

In Northern Ireland the Catholics tried to break away from the predominantly Protestant United Kingdom. Ireland has a long history (including prehistory) of being invaded. Shortly after the Normans conquered England they set their sights on Ireland too. As they were invading Ireland from their newly conquered England this is usually written up as the first English claim over Ireland. In 1177 Prince John Lackland was made Lord of Ireland by his father Henry II of England at the Council of Oxford. This marked the beginning of more than 800 years of direct English rule. At this time both countries were, of course, Catholic.

Then in 1688 began the Williamite War in Ireland (1688-1691). This was a conflict between Jacobites (supporters of the Catholic King James II of England and Ireland, VII of Scotland) and Williamites (supporters of the Dutch Protestant Prince William of Orange) over who would be monarch of the Kingdom of England, the Kingdom of Scotland and the Kingdom of Ireland. The origins of the Irish Republican Army (IRA) are rather obscure but probably date from the Fenian raids on many

British towns, and forts in the late 1700s. Whatever you may think of their methods the IRA is a response to the English (Protestant) occupation of their country. People everywhere want self rule and who can blame them. The USSR fell apart. Yugoslavia fell apart. The trend is clearly away from globalism towards independent, self governing nations. Let's not buck that trend.

The *existence* of countries does not cause wars. What causes war is people disrespecting the boarders and the sovereignty of other nations. Actually it goes deeper than that. What really causes wars is the greed of arms manufacturers who want to sell weapons to both sides, the greed of bankers who want to lend both sides the money to buy those weapons, and the corrupt politicians and media barons who get back handers for stirring up the public to believe its alright to disrespect the boarders and the sovereignty of other nations. Don't get rid of countries, address the real problem instead, the globalist elite.

In the Middle East, Israel has become a nation once again and its Muslim neighbours are also splitting apart along ethnic and religious lines. The region had been carved up between Britain and France following the First World War with scant regard for the religious and ethnic sensibilities of the native people. Such artificial countries cannot last. They inevitably split up into smaller units sooner or later.

This is exactly what happened in India with the splitting away of Pakistan and Bangladesh. Its nothing to do with prejudice or racism. Its just that people like to live among people with similar customs and values to themselves and they like their leaders to share those customs and values too. Its perfectly normal and healthy. That's why multiculturalism doesn't work. This is why in multicultural countries such as, for example, Britain and Sweden, the different cultures only mix to a very limited extent and unofficial *nations within nations* have developed along religious and ethnic lines. The truth is that multiculturalism doesn't work. It never will work. It was a disastrous idea from the start. The inevitable trend is towards a greater number of small, self-governing countries.

We must stop invading other peoples' countries, with or without weapons, because, sooner or later, all conquered people rebel and take their territory back. Even when, as in the case of Israel, it takes them many hundreds of years and the help of more powerful nations. Nobody has the right, ever, to go to another country and demand that the locals change their way of life. Immigrants into Europe, America and Australia have no right to make such demands and Western governments have no right to send troops into Iraq, Libya or Syria and try to affect regime change. We must respect the sovereignty of other countries and their people must respect ours. That's what countries are for.

There are currently nearly 200 different countries in the world, each with its own unique set of customs and laws which suit the people who live there. It would be a good thing if more split apart to give even more variety and choice and to best serve the needs of the inhabitants.

Freedom, Variety and Choice - It is, or at least should be, all about freedom, variety and choice. Wouldn't it be great if people were free to choose whichever county suited their needs the best and were free to move there? But only if they move there because they love it there, just the way it is. Newcomers have no right to start making changes. In fact first generation immigrants should not even have the right to vote or to hold public office. You don't move to someone else's' country and then start telling them what they can and can't do. That's just plain bad manners. If you don't love the place, just the way it is, you have no business being there.

Contrast this with the *newspeak* coming from so-called *progressive* sources. *Progressives* are not the good, liberal, open-minded people they pretend to be. Theirs is a *globalist* agenda designed to take away our last vestiges of freedom, variety and choice. They want an impoverished planet where there is just one world culture, ruled over by an unaccountable, totalitarian world government. Make no mistake, bringing about such a dystopian New World Order is the remit of the United Nations. But they will fail and we will win by looking after one another and by following the suggestions laid before you here in this book.

And some people need religion too. Science explains a lot but it leaves many questions unanswered. People still seek these answers and when science lets them down they turn to more intuitive methods of inquiry.

There is a Hindu proverb that says *There are hundreds of paths up the mountain, all leading to the same place, so it doesn't matter which path you take. The only person wasting time is the one who runs around the mountain, telling everyone else that his or her path is wrong.*

Modern Pagans put it more succinctly when they say *All paths lead to the centre.* Actually I prefer *All tolerant paths lead to the centre* because it seems to me that bigoted religions that preach hatred and intolerance are leading their followers away from the centre, back down the mountain.

Religion is about more than just seeking answers to life's deepest questions. Religious practice enriches people's lives in a similar way to art. If people practice their religion peacefully, enjoy it, get something out of it, and don't try to force it down other people's throats, what right do unbelievers have to try and ban it?

We hear the globalists complaining that religion causes war but that's a nonsense argument. It is not religion but bigotry and intolerance that lead to religious wars so don't ban religion, ban bigotry and intolerance. Or better still, don't ban these things, such a ban would never work. Much better to remove their root cause which is fear. And that, dear reader, is precisely what this book is all about. Religious wars are seldom about what they appear to be about anyway. Only the foot solders believe that. The politicians and generals are just after power and world leaders may allegedly be in the pay of the international arms dealers. And the media barons, such as Rupert Murdoch and the BBC, need to be on side to brainwash the populace into supporting the war. I wonder what inducements they are getting for playing along in this deadliest of games.

Its not all carrots of course. There are also sticks for those who refuse to co-operate with the war machine. Just look at what happened to Dr. David Kelly. He was a distinguished UK government scientist who hunted down weapons of mass destruction (WMDs). Blair and Bush depended on the lie of Iraq possessing WMDs in order to justify their illegal war. The problem was the Saddam Hussein government did not have any and Kelly spilt the beans to the BBC *Today* programme. He was called to testify before a parliamentary committee where he was aggressively questioned about his role in the scandal. He was found dead two days later.

On 18th July 2003 his body was found dead on Harrowdown Hill, near his home in Longworth, Oxfordshire. His death was ruled a suicide by the judicial inquiry chaired by Lord Hutton, but was it just too convenient? He had no reason to take his own life and the British government had every reason to want him dead. So was Dr. Kelly murdered on the orders of Her Majesty's Government? We will never know for sure.

What we do know is his death was not the fault of the existence of countries or religions although it could have been caused by greed, lust for power and corruption at the highest level.

How much better it would have been, how much closer to utopia it would have brought us, had Lennon encouraged us to imagine a world where different countries and different religions co-operate with each other in a spirit of love and tolerance. But I suppose it wouldn't have made for such a catchy song.

Nationalism - Let's take a closer look at nationalism. Nationalism is often portrayed as being narrow-minded and inward looking while Globalism is seen as broad-minded and outward looking, but is this right? John Lennon seemed to think so when he asked us to imagine a world without separate countries. Then again, he was probably unaware of how big and powerful multi-national corporations were to become. Many are more powerful and have more influence than democratically elected governments, so powerful in fact that they can get away without paying their taxes for years. He must also have been quite ignorant of history.

I said at the start of this book that my vision for a fairer world is neither left wing nor right wing but a synthesis of the best of both philosophies. Some people call me a nationalist and maybe I am although I tend to resist all predefined labels. Other people call me an anarchist so maybe I am that too. As I say, I'm not easy to categorise.

I need to make it clear that whenever I talk about Nationalism in this book I am using the term solely to mean the opposite of Globalism. That's it. I am not talking about about *my country is better than your country* or *my religion is better than your religion* or *my race is better than your race* or any of that old nonsense. I just want what all true liberals want, decentralised decision making. Any political party that does not want decentralised decision making is not a true liberal party, regardless of what it calls itself.

Throughout history globalists have tried to *unite* the world. Fantastic! At least until we realise that what they really want is to unite the world under *their* leadership. Hitler's ambition was to unite Europe and ultimately the world, under his control. EU leaders have a similar ambition today.

The Roman Empire was an attempt to unify the known world, under Roman control of course.

Alfred the Great wanted to unite all the Kingdoms of England (the name the Saxons used for the territory they had recently conquered from the British) under his control.

Alexander the Great wanted to unite the known world of his day under his control.

And Napoleon Bonaparte was another despotic globalist psychopath with the same age old ambition.

Now its the turn of the totalitarian E.U.

When will we ever learn to see through the globalist

propaganda? We can be sure that if ever we do end up with a world government it will not be a democracy, rather it will be rich globalist elite, from the world of banking, business and politics, lording it over the rest of us.

Back in the 1970s and 80s Greens and Liberals understood that free speech, tolerance, decentralisation, short, local supply lines and self-sufficiency were the way to a sustainable future. Then, somehow, both the green and liberal movements became infiltrated by globalists and our dream was dashed.

Well I used to be a proud green and a proud liberal, back in the days when those labels still meant sustainability, tolerance, free speech and freedom. How did we lose our way?

Now I am proud to be a nationalist.

We nationalists want to live in a free and independent country and, by extension, we want every other country in the world to be free and independent too.

We want a world filled with free and independent nations, all different, all special and all co-operating together willingly.

We respect other people's national boundaries and we demand that they respect ours.

We respect other countries' cultures and we demand that

they respect ours.

Foreigners are welcome to live among us provided they adapt to our way of life and do not expect us to change to suit them.

We don't start wars or invade other people's countries, that's globalists.

Globalism, with its one size fits all solutions, doesn't work.

Nationalists are the true greens because we want decentralisation, short, local supply lines and self-sufficiency.

Nationalists are the true liberals because we want freedom of speech, the freedom to debate on all subjects and the freedom for everyone to do their own thing without having to worry about *offending* intolerant idiots.

We want freedom of religion for everyone within the limits set by law (there has to be limits, we can't allow human sacrifice for instance). Everyone should be free to practice their own beliefs, peacefully, within the confines of the law of the land. And everyone must have the right to change their beliefs and to leave any religion at any time.

We want equality for every citizen regardless of race, religion or gender and we understand that equality includes taking equal responsibility for the consequences of our actions.

We want national governments to make their countries' laws, laws which suit their citizens' needs, their culture and their traditions. We must never permit foreign laws or foreign courts to operate in our country , whether the European Court of Justice or Sharia courts.

Nationalism, freedom, individuality, equality and respect pave the road to a better future, not dull, suffocating globalism.

Nationalists want more co-operation, but co-operation between free, independent nations.

One of the most important aspects of what could be called Enlightened Liberal Nationalism is the right of all nations to self-determination. The right to self-determination is entrenched as a norm within the governance of any liberal democracy, and the desire to determine one's own territorial boundaries remains an immensely powerful driving force within international relations.

We firmly oppose imperialism and insist on mutual respect for the independence of all sovereign nations.

The European Union is failing precisely because it tried to take away the independence of member states. Indeed, calling them *states* rather than *nations* should have warned us of their federal ambitions.

As I said above, it will soon be time to establish the European Network of Free and Independent Nations (ENFIN). No political union, just free trade, friendship and co-operation and its up to us to lead the way.

Beware of political censorship, the repression of ideas. So-called *political correctness* is an Orwellian tool invented by totalitarian globalists to suppress free speech and open discussion and we must reject it absolutely. Its a tool used by elites to control the people. One of it's nastiest weapons is so-called *hate speech* legislation where the emotive word *hate* is used to mean all legitimate criticism.

Speaking of George Orwell, he invented the concept of *new-speak* where everything is backwards. Well today everything is backwards. The free speech hating fascists who insist on *political correctness* are now coming from the left, not the right and their Brownshirts call themselves Antifa and pretend to be anti-Nazi. But their definition of Nazi is anyone further to the right than themselves. The truth is that they, themselves, are the true Nazis of today, violently attacking anyone who stands for freedom and equality.

We most certainly do not think that our race or skin colour or religion makes us superior to anyone else. Please don't confuse nationalists with white supremacists or black supremacists or Muslim supremacists or Christian supremacists or any other kind of supremacists. We are none of those things. We are nationalists. We

71

want to see lots of small, devolved, independent nations where each of those groups can find a home, where people can live with others who share common values, common beliefs, common assumptions and a common culture.

Multiculturalism is a failed experiment. People like to live among their own kind. And people have the right to insist that newcomers adapt themselves and try to fit in. Most people welcome immigrants who make an effort to learn the culture and blend in seamlessly. Genuine migrants move to a foreign country with the intention of allowing it to change them. If you go to a country, with or without guns, with the intention of changing it, you are an invader, not an immigrant.

Nationalism, freedom, individuality, universal equality and respect for the differences that make us all special pave the road to Utopia - not dull, suffocating one-size-fits-all globalism.

Migrants really should be Citizens of the World

Wouldn't it be great if we could all move freely around a world with no borders? Yes it wound and when we all learn to travel with respect for the people who where there before us, for their culture and traditions, we can make that world a reality. But it will never happen while our arrival drives fear into the hearts of the native people, fear that the land they call home will be changed beyond recognition forever. So shall we build a new world where there is nothing to be afraid of? Shall we build a world rooted in Love Not Fear?

Migration isn't the problem. The way we currently do migration is the problem. But we can change that. We must change that.

If we were to ban all immigration we could never live abroad ourselves. We would have to accept imprisonment in our own land.

If you prefer the culture in another country of course you should be free to move there and embrace it. What people must never be permitted to do is move to a foreign country and impose their culture on their new neighbours. When I talk about culture here I am not referring to things like your choice of food or music. I am talking about fundamental cultural values such as freedom, free speech, freedom of religion and gender equality. If you don't believe in these things, then please don't move to a country where people do. Likewise, if you do believe in these things, don't move to a country where such views are not welcome.

I can't believe that people who have been brainwashed with *newspeak* call me a racist for saying these things. This philosophy is the very opposite of racism. This philosophy is rooted in Universal Equality and respect for all people regardless of race, religion or gender. And it is rooted in the founding principles of Love Not Fear where we try not to scare the crap out of each other. Multiethnic is fine but multiculturalism will never work.

I really do want to build a world where people will be free to travel and indeed settle anywhere they wish provided they come with love in their hearts and follow the first pillar of Utopia, be excellent to each-other. Be excellent especially to the established population whose families may well have lived there for hundreds or even thousands of years. Show them respect, obey their laws and fully integrate into their culture. Surely that's not too much to ask.

Relocate because you don't like where you are living, for whatever reason, and you believe another country would suit you better. Nothing wrong with that. So why are so many people moving into Britain, Europe, America, Canada, Australia and New Zeeland hell bent on turning their new country into a replica of the place they just left? Doesn't make any sense.

Migration is when you go to country with the intention of being changed by it. Invasion is when you go to a country with the intention of changing that country. What the world needs now is more migrants and fewer invaders (with or without guns and bombs).

There are nearly two hundred different countries on this planet, each with its own unique set of laws and traditions. Surely that's enough choice for everyone. But there is only one legitimate reason to want to live in a foreign country and that reason is that you love that country, every aspect of that country, just the way it is. At the very least, you must be prepared to put up with any aspects you don't like without making a fuss.

Now please don't think I am against migration or against migrants. I most certainly am not. I have lived nearly half my adult life as a migrant, 3 years in The Netherlands and 17 years in Spain. I have been with the best, most respectful of migrants and I have also been with the very worst, rude, arrogant people who made me ashamed to be British.

When I returned to England in 2012 I lived in a part of Oxford which had many migrants. Once again I saw the very best as well as the very worst of immigrants.

I am passionate about making migration work and my experiences mean that I can now see the way forward and I sharing my insights with you here.

People have no right to move just for a better climate, while hating the local culture, as many Brits are doing right now in Spain. Most love the climate and the culture of course, learn the language to the best of their ability and really try to fit in. I lived 17 years in Spain and ran a business there. Sure there were aspects of the Spanish system I found challenging but they were a small price to pay for the privilege of living there.

And in today's distopian world some countries are richer than others. There are many economic migrants moving to the richer countries. But people have absolutely no right to move for purely financial reasons with absolutely no intention of fully integrating into the local culture. And they have absolutely no right to try and bring their own sharia laws with them either. If you want to live in a country then obey that country's laws and leave your old country's laws behind.

I am very much in favour of the free movement of people but it has to be done properly. The way it is currently being implemented in many parts of the world is a nightmare. The whole idea of multiculturalism is a globalist disaster. It has led to resentment and hatred everywhere it has been tried. Migrants must adopt the host culture, that's the only way this migration thing is ever ever going to work

Migrants are quick enough to accuse their hosts of racism while being exceedingly slow to ask themselves if their own bad behaviour or bad attitude is the cause of it. In my experience there is very little genuine racism in the world and a lot of justifiable resistance to arrogant migrants who don't know how to behave abroad.

Newcomers have absolutely no right to try and change their adopted country. To do so would be disrespectful and would most certainly not be being excellent to the established population there. Entering a country in order to change it is an invasion, not a migration.

If you do not love your new country just the way it is, or at least tolerate the bits you don't like, you have no right to be there.

Of course migrants can keep their own religion. The seventh pillar of utopia, Freedom of Religion, guarantees

76

that, so long as they practice it unobtrusively and respect the freedom of religion of those who believe differently.

When in Rome do as the Romans do - This sound advice was given to St. Augustine back in the 4th century and is just as valid now as it was then. When visiting a foreign land, follow the customs of those who live in it. It can also mean that when you are in an unfamiliar situation, you should follow the lead of those who know the ropes. This doesn't mean you can't eat your favourite food or listen to your favourite music, of course not. Be free, be an individual, have fun. Just try not to piss off the locals.

Multiculturalism is a failed experiment. National borders exist to contain and protect cultures. If you don't like the culture where you are living, move, you are not a tree. There are nearly 200 different countries to choose from. Go where you will be happiest.

Trying to run different, often incompatible cultures along side each other in the same place is a recipe for disaster. When the newcomers choose to live and dress the same way as their hosts harmony can be quickly restored. I am certainly not telling anyone how to behave or dress (within accepted limits). This must be the free choice of every individual but choices have consequences and people must be willing to accept the consequences of their choices. It may be that choosing not to fit in will result in friction with the local people. If you chose not to fit in then you caused that.

Travel broadens the mind so when you move allow your mind to be stretched and enriched by new ideas. Don't take your old narrow-minded attitudes with you.

Now please don't get the wrong end of the stick here. I am absolutely, absolutely, absolutely NOT trying to tell people how to dress. That would be totally inappropriate. It would also be compliantly against the whole theme of this book which is about freedom, freedom of speech, freedom of expression and freedom from the game we did not devise.

It would be awful if we were all the same, just a bunch of soleless clones walking around. Sure we are all one but we are all unique, individual expressions of the one Universal Mind and we must be free to express our individuality any way we chose.

Be free, be brash if yo want to be, be colourful, be you. Reveal as much as you want. Conceal as much as you want (provided you leave your face viable for security reasons). Enjoy the music you love and the food you love.

When I talk about newcomers adopting the host culture I mean the underlying, fundamental cultural values, not how you dress, eat or enjoy yourself. You are a beautiful, unique butterfly so fly!

I have spoken elsewhere in this book about *good migrants* and *bad migrants* based on how they behave and how much effort they put into adapting and fitting in. Please don't think I am necessarily blaming the migrants. Its true that some just come here to make trouble but many have never been abroad before and have no idea how to behave.

Rather than blame them can we please try to show them love and help them to integrate. The host nations are as much to blame as the bad migrants. We tell them our countries are *multicultural* so they don't need to integrate. We must stop telling them that.

Indeed we should be allocating each new arrival a social worker, maybe called an *integration officer* to help them blend in. There to help without judging for the first year but then responsible for making a *Sufficient Progress Report* on the basis of which the migrant will be allowed to stay or be repatriated.

This is one example of what can happen when migrants are neither expected or helped to assimilate into the host culture. In March 2017 Birmingham councillor Waseem Zaffar claimed that St. Clare's Catholic Primary School had breached anti-discrimination laws by refusing to allow a four year old girl to wear a Muslim headscarf.

However he had it all backwards. There was no discrimination. The 'no hats or headwear' rule applied equally to all pupils regardless of race, religion or gender.

Rather than arguing against discrimination, Zaffar was actually asking for discrimination in favour of Muslims.

Here is another UK example. A London coroner who refused to let Jewish and Muslim burials jump the queue was accused in the High Court of breaching human rights because she stood up for human rights and equally. You couldn't make this stuff up.

Two religious groups brought a legal challenge against a policy established by Mary Hassell, the senior coroner for inner north London. She had been dealing with the deaths in her jurisdiction on a first-come, first-served basis.

Jewish and Muslim groups argued that their dead should be buried first, because of their beliefs. Mary Hassell maintained that everyone should be treated equally, regardless of their religion. On the 27th April 2018, in the High Court, Sikh judge Lord Justice Singh and Mrs. Justice Whipple decreed that the *equality protocol* policy to be *unlawful, irrational and discriminatory*. Yes you read that correctly. An equally protocol has be ruled as being discriminatory because it refused to discriminate.

Britain, like many other western countries, is now being led by bigoted racist idiots who hate the native people whose families have been here for hundreds of years. They think they are being clever but all they are doing is stoking up more and ever more resentment against the immigrants.

Of course people from hot countries have a tradition of quick burial. They don't want bodies lying around stinking. I lived in Spain for 17 years. The Christians there have a similar tradition, and for exactly the same reason. But they are not in a hot country now, they are here, so they should adopt our traditions.

Because of the climate Spanish bin lorries call every day. So following the logic of this decision, should immigrants from hot countries get their bins emptied more often than everyone else? I don't think so.

Here's a great idea. I am an old codger now so maybe I will start a new religion, the Church of Codger. The main tenant of our faith is that we are entitled to twice the old age pension of everyone else. I would love to take that before the same two stupid judges just to see how consistent they would be. Britain needs a law making it illegal for anyone to discriminate against, or in favour of, any person or group on the basis of their race, religion or gender.

Actually we already have such a law, The Equally Act (2010) but it is only being applied selectively. Government must give instructions to the courts that they have to treat everyone the same regardless of race, religion or gender.

We get this so often now, newcomers demanding racist exemptions to our rules and laws and accusing us of racism when we refuse to bow to their racism. Its all backwards, its Orwellian *newspeak*.

Tolerance is backwards too these days - It used to mean everyone getting along and being free to be themselves. Now its supposed to be intolerant to *offend* intolerant people. Excuse me. Tolerant people are not easily offended and intolerant people are not welcome.

People never used to be so easily offended, we all used to have thicker skins.

In a fair society, the same rules and laws must apply to everyone regardless of race, religion or gender. And when people move to a new country they must obey all the rules and laws of that country and fully integrate into its culture.

If they are not willing and eager to do that they have no right to be there.

There will be a few of you, I know, who will not bother to try and understand what I have actually written here. They will jump to false conclusions based on their own prejudices and accuse me of racism. This happens far too often.

For the benefit of those people let me state, for the record, that the same *When in Rome* rule must apply to everyone, regardless of race, religion or gender.

In this chapter I have given an example of a Muslim failing to apply this rule.

Let me give a few other examples of this rule being broken.

The British invasion of Ireland.

The British invasion of India.

The European invasion of the Americas.

The British invasion of Australia.

The British military reaction to the closure of the Suiz Canal.

The Dutch and British invasion of South Africa.

The British / French carve up of the Middle East following the First World War.

The American invasion of Iraq (twice).

The American invasion of Afghanistan.

The American invasion of Lybia.

All the American covert operations by their CIA to effect regime change in foreign countries.

These are just a few of the many times that white European and American people have interfered in other people's countries. Its not just brown skinned people doing this.

Never invade other peoples' countries. There's no telling

how it will end.

There is absolutely nothing racist about my position. The same rules must apply to everyone regardless of race, religion or gender.

I am very much a product of the liberal attitudes of the 1960s, before the Liberals and Greens were infiltrated by globalists.

My liberal attitude to race and immigration was greatly influenced by the 1969 song, *Melting Pot*.

Melting Pot was the debut single from the British band *Blue Mink*. The song was written by Blue Mink's lead singer Roger Cook and long-time songwriter partner Roger Greenaway.

Melting Pot Lyrics -

Take a pinch of white man
Wrap it up in black skin
Add a touch of blue blood
And a little bitty bit of Red Indian boy

Curly Latin kinkies
Mixed with yellow Chinkees
If you lump it all together
Well, you got a recipe for a get along scene
Oh, what a beautiful dream

If it could only come true, you know, you know

What we need is a great big melting pot
Big enough to take the world and all it's got
And keep it stirring for a hundred years or more
And turn out coffee coloured people by the score

Rabbis and the Friars
Vishnus and the Gurus
You got the Beatles or the Sun God, it's true
Well, it really doesn't matter what religion you
choose
No, no no

Making Lady Favour
Mrs. Graceful
You know that living could be tasteful
We should all get together in a loving machine
I better call up the Queen
It's only fair that she knows, you know, you know

What we need is a great big melting pot
Big enough to take the world and all it's got
And keep it stirring for a hundred years or more
And turn out coffee coloured people by the score

What we need, what we need is a great big melting
pot
Big enough, big enough, big enough

To take the world and all it's got
And keep it stirring for a hundred years or more
And turn out coffee coloured people by the score

What we need is a great big melting pot
Big enough, big enough, big enough
To take the world and all it's got
And keep it stirring for a hundred years or more
And turn out coffee coloured people by the score

What a beautiful dream. It could almost have happened, almost. But then some idiot thought up the disastrous concept of *multiculturalism*.

Suddenly we no longer needed a melting pot because people were being told they could settle anywhere on the planet they wanted without having to adopt the local culture and integrate. What a disaster.

Migrants could bring their old culture with them and in some cases their own laws too, Sharia Law. They could live in ghettos and establish their own state within a state. How crazy is that? But don't you dare speak out against it or the loonies will brand you a racist or even a fascist. But indeed many brave people are speaking out against it despite being wrongly branded as *racists* and *fascists*, which of course they are not.

So another crazy concept had to be invented to try to silence them, *Political Correctness* and the associated term *Hate Speech*. Censorship by another name. George Orwell must be turning over in his grave.

All this hate speech nonsense is getting out of hand now. It has nothing to do with the prevention of violence. Incitement to violence has always been illegal and should always be prosecuted. We don't need hate speech laws.

People are now being sent to prison for speaking the truth on social media under Hate Speech laws. George Orwell most certainly in writhing in his grave now.

Funny thing about Hate Speech laws. If you criticise, quite fairly, quite truthfully, the things an immigrant or group of immigrants are actually doing its called *Hate Speech*. But if your opponents want to call you hateful, misleading names such as *racist* or *fascist* or even *Nazi*, that is never classified as Hate Speech. Funny that. Even more funny that they are totally blind to their own double standards.

Hate speech laws are even being used to silence honest criticism of political groups, such as Political Islam. I am all for respecting other people's religions but any group that wants to change our laws or introduce a set of foreign laws, such as Sharia law, is practicing politics not religion. How did we ever allow this to happen? How did we ever allow the creation, in our midsts, of a group of people who are above criticism? Its crazy.

Of course there is nothing wrong with the established

population learning from the newcomers. The important thing is for the settlers to introduce their ideas gently and be willing to take no for an answer if their ideas are not welcome.

***Cultural Transmission, Cultural Enrichment* and *Cultural Appropriation* -** When I was at university we were taught about *Cultural Transmission*, the process through which cultural elements, in the form of attitudes, values, beliefs, and behaviour, are passed from one culture to another.

Then, in an attempt to pacify resistance to uncontrolled, mass migration, another term was introduced, *Cultural Enrichment*. This is when migrants enrich the lives of the host population by bringing such things as their their food, music and dance with them.

Of course not everything they bring is enriching. FGM, religious intolerance, gender inequality and gender segregation are most certainly not enriching. This is why the host population must have the right to choose which elements to be enriched by and which to reject.

Then in the last couple of years a really backward concept was introduced, *Cultural Appropriation*. According to this very racist theory the newcomers have the right to decide which parts of their culture the host population are permitted to be enriched by. *Cultural Appropriation* is a total denial of both *Cultural Transmission* and *Cultural Enrichment*.

Why do the so-called *progressives* call it *cultural enrichment* when newcomers try to force their ideas on us but *cultural appropriation* when we actually embrace any of those ideas? Is it just me or can anyone else see the double standards going on here?

While on the subject - Why do the so-called *progressives* want us to take responsibility for the mistakes our ancestors made before we were born but throw a fit when we show any pride in the good things our ancestors did?

And, come to that, why do they call it *whitewashing* when a white actor plays an originally non-white character while calling for Idris Elba to play James Bond? Why is that not criticised as *blackwashing*?

We are clearly being conned here.

The same rules must apply to everyone regardless of race, religion or gender. So if its okay for a black fellow to have dreadlocks or play soul music or whatever it happens to be then its equally okay for everyone else on the planet to do the same thing, regardless of race, religion or gender. Appropriate whatever you like, its called *freedom* !

The same thing applies to the use of the *N* word. Personalty I would like to see it disappear altogether but to say one race can do something that another race cannot is the very definition of racism.

Let's not lose sight of what we are trying to achieve here. This isn't about knocking migrants. We are trying to find a way to move towards a utopian society where freedom of movement will be the norm, where we can all be proud, responsible citizens of the world. But in order to achieve that we must establish a set of ground rules whereby newcomers can be quickly and seamlessly absorbed into the established population of their chosen country. What I am proposing here is a set of such ground rules.

We will achieve a state of utopia when we all have good manners, when we all respect one another, when we are all excellent to one another. And that's the only way this migration thing is going to work too.

Migrants will only be welcome if they have good manners, if they respect the established population and are excellent to them. Only then will the migrants themselves be respected We really can live in Love Not Fear, we just have to choose to do so.

CHAPTER SEVEN - Fair people-centric government

The people of each country must be free to choose the type of government they wish.

I am British so I tend to write about the type of government I want in the United Kingdom. It is not my wish to try and impose this anywhere else.

Many forms of government have been tried around the world since our species began. The strongest male chimp is usually the leader who rules with the help of other strong, mature males.

As we evolved, our tribes were similarly ruled and as our tribes got bigger we had kings, czars and emperors. Up until the middle ages, kings would lead their armies into battle. They earned their privileged position. Then they got lazy and claimed that the divine right of kings gave them their power. Unrest among the people stirred.

Various alternative governments were tried in different places. Russian communism gained public support by offering to bring power to the people. But the new government turned out to be just as cruel and greedy as the czar had been and it soon became apparent that *the people* was just a euphemism for *the government*. People had simply replaced one oppressor for another.

To achieve world peace we must look deeper than the old straight line left - right - centre model of politics.

The old, straight line, left - right - centre model of politics would have you believe that Stalin and Hitler where opposites whereas in actual fact they were very similar people with very similar totalitarian beliefs.

Both wanted to rule the people with an iron grip. Both opposed free speech and both incarcerated or murdered those who opposed them.

Indeed both claimed to be socialists but were in reality fascists who opposed free speech and civil liberties.

Perhaps it's time to abandon the old model. For a while I toyed with a circular model where both extremes meet in the centre. However I now prefer a straight line model with all freedom loving parties on the right, and the far right position taken by anarchists. That way moderate socialists can remain on the left with all totalitarian parties, both communist and fascist, on the far left.

Ultimately, of course, all political parties want the same thing, they want more people to rule over, they want more power.

To achieve peace we need a brand new paradigm, a totally new way to think about politics. A lot of people who yearn for utopia, me included, dream of anarchy. Wouldn't it be great to have no leaders and for everyone to do the right thing simply because it is the right thing? Yes it would but we are not ready for that yet. Sure it can work on a small scale, on a commune say, but there are too many selfish, greedy people in the world for anarchy to work on a large scale. Another thousand years perhaps?

Or perhaps not quite that long. As I suggested at the start of this book, hurt people hurt people and frightened people act in desperate ways. Maybe if we can find a way to stop hurting and scaring each other, by following the ideas in this book, we could build a society based on love, generosity, or at least enlightened self interest, where anarchy could be possible. What do you think?

We may not be ready for total anarchy quite yet but whatever system of government we choose, let's make it as light and unobtrusive as possible. Laws should be kept to the bare minimum and people should be free to run their own lives as they wish as long as they are being excellent to each-other and to Mother Earth.

Whatever system we choose, I hope it will be a truly democratic one. It must be fair and it must treat everyone the same, regardless of race, religion or gender. It must also support free speech for without free and open debate on all subjects, solutions to problems can never be found. Censorship and political correctness just leave resentments simmering under the surface until they boil over into violence.

In the beginning was the Elite and the Elite were few and the people were many.

And darkness spread into the souls of the Elite.

And the Elite yearned to rule the people with an iron fist, yet the people resisted.

So the Elite dreamt up a plan.

And the Elite spoke with one voice and said *let us have the illusion of democracy to fool the people. Let there be two political parties and let the people swear allegiance to one or the other and let them fight and argue for all eternity, and let them be so distracted by their bickering that they never realise that we, the Elite, control both parties.*

BUT IT DOESN'T HAVE TO BE THIS WAY

We have the technology, we can rebuild our democracy, we really can.

Democracy - the government of the people by the people where the will of the majority prevails. Wouldn't that be nice?

In Britain we have a system where each town or district, called a 'constituency' has the right to send a representative to speak in Parliament on behalf of the local people. At least that's the theory. In practice,

94

parliamentary seats have always been stitched up among a limited number of political parties and members of parliament (MPs) tend to represent their parties before their constituents.

Political parties are rather like trade unions that MPs join, so as to gang up against their constituents. You have probably never thought about it that way before but I invite you to do so now.

We are all familiar with one party systems, the old USSR, North Korea and Communist China for example, where people can vote for any candidate they choose so long as he or she stands for the sole ruling Communist Party. Such countries call themselves 'democracies' although they don't seem very democratic to you and me.

Make it a two party state and you have doubled the choice and doubled the level of democracy. Make it a four party state and democracy doubles once again. Carrying this on to its logical conclusion, image a country that has the same number of parties as it has MPs. Then each MP would be independent and free to represent his or her constituents. You would have a very democratic system indeed.

But can we devise a system that is even more democratic than that? I think that, with the aid of modern technology, we can.

Every day in Britain, and around the world, millions of safe, secure chip and pin financial transactions take place. A few go wrong but only a miniscule percentage. Let's apply the same technology to our democratic process. Let's give every registered voter a chip and pin type poling card and let's put voting machines in every public building, Then everybody who chose to could vote in every debate in the House of Commons. There would need to be a delay of a couple of days after the debate before the vote to give people time to follow it on TV and to do their own research.

Of course most people would not have the time or the interest to participate in every vote. That's fine. That's what we have MPs for. Each MP would be able to cast as many votes as they have registered voters in their constituency LESS the number who chose to vote for themselves in that particular debate. Its child's play to write computer code to calculate that. Most 15 year olds could do it.

Just think about it, instead of being fobbed off with a token vote every five years or so, you could vote in every parliamentary debate that you had an interest in. Now that's what I call democracy.

There would have to be a couple of conditions. People would have to agree to stand by the democratic will of the people. There could be no demands for a second vote if the result doesn't go your way. If we could do that we would just go around in circles for ever. Just follow the debate, vote, then move on to the next issue.

No votes for prison inmates. Follow that to its logical

conclusion and you could imagine some future where there would be enough inmates that they could vote to make their crime legal or vote to close all prisons. That would just be absurd.

And thirdly, and most controversially, no votes for first generation immigrants. Let people be free to live in any country they choose, where the laws and customs are to their liking, but don't let them move to a place where the laws and customs are not to their liking and then start making changes. That would just be crazy. If they don't like the way we do thing here, why come?

We really must stop bickering among ourselves. Its not the ordinary people who are to blame, left, right, centre, we are all on the same side. If there is an enemy it is the ruling classes, the ones who pretend there are different political parties in order to divide us and rule us.

Anarchists sometimes accuse me of being a *statist* when I mention the benefits of national governments but that's not the case at all. I long for the time when we can do away with all governments and all borders, but we are not there yet. In the meantime I would much rather have lots of small independent nations, each with its own government, than one totally out of control, totalitarian world government. I am sure you will agree that that would be a disaster, but that would be the inevitable result were we to just scrap our borders before we had made the necessary preparations as described in the pages of this book. We can get there, we will get there, but we have to be smart.

We will still need governments for a few more years but we must never let our politicians have too much power. Remember our history. Remember how Hitler's strong government told the people what they were and were not allowed to say and what they were and were not allowed to think.

We must never again let any government become more powerful than the people.

We must never again allow any government to do our thinking for us or tell us what we may or may not say or think. We must reject political correctness and the increasingly totalitarian EU superstate at all costs. Keep nations small and independent, small enough to have real democracies where the ordinary people make the important decisions.

The voice of the people must be heard over the voices of politicians and the establishment. It makes no difference which party is in office. What matters is how much control over our lives we give away to politicians and how much we keep for ourselves.

They will tell us that can't work, that we are too stupid to think for ourselves, or the real beauty, the absolute peach, which goes something like this - politicians lie to us so only they can recognise their own lies, so best let them make all our decisions for us.

Excuse me. Are you really saying that dishonest

politicians should make our decisions for us because politicians are dishonest ? Isn't that like chasing a burglar down the street, carrying your family jewels in your hand, shouting "excuse me mate, I think you forgot these".

Wouldn't it be better to stop them from lying to us in the first place ? How's this for an idea - how about when we catch the bastards lying to us, we stop voting for them ? Surely lying politicians are a reason to take power away from them, not give them more. Lying politicians and the lying media barons they are in cahoots with are the problem, not the solution.

Will you stand with us and help bring us one step closer to utopia? I hope that you will.

The Return of Totalitarianism In the first edition of this book I called this section *The Return of Fascism*. Then people started writing in and we got into a silly argument about whether fascism is far left or far right. The point of course is that it really doesn't matter. Fascism and Communism are just different forms of Totalitarianism.

The greatest con trick of our time has been enacted by globalists and totalitarians against the people.

Anti-totalitarians have been conned into believing that there are both far right and far left totalitarian groups when really they are all the same. That's why we see groups like Antifa behaving exactly like Hitler Brown

99

Shirts, while believing themselves to be anti-fascist. What a sick joke!

Rather than setting the so-called far left and the so-called far right against each other we need to set all the freedom loving people of the world against all forms of totalitarianism.

As mentioned earlier we need a new model of politics that puts all totalitarian regimes together on the far left and freedom on the right

A simpler way of saying this would be strong government / weak people on the left, weak government / strong people on the right, Or the other way around. The allocation of 'left' and 'right' here is quite arbitrary.

Never again must any government be permitted to become stronger than the people it is supposed to represent.

And never again can we tolerate any politicians who take the attitude that they know what's best for the people.

I have nothing against true liberals, indeed I am one myself, but I have no time for fake liberals. The word liberal has the same root as liberty. True liberals believe in liberty and freedom, freedom of speech and freedom of expression. They also believe in Universal Equality. Fake liberals, on the other hand, hate freedom. They want to control what other people are allowed to say, do and think with their accursed political correctness and no-performing. Fake liberals are really fascists in disguise. Beware of fake liberals.

Having made that clear, here is the rest of the section as originally written.

Everyone needs to know this. We have been systematically lied to since 1944. We have been fed a big fat lie and we need to know the truth.

We deserve to know the truth that Hitler and Mussolini were Marxists. Fascism, and later Nazism, grew out of Marxism. It may shock you to hear that but please don't take my word for it. Do your own research. Here follows a very brief account of the birth of fascism. The reason we need to look at this ugly subject here is so we can recognise it when we see it in our modern world, and not be taken in by it. Things may not be as they first appear or as we have been programmed to believe. The world is experiencing a dangerous resurgence of fascism and we must all stand firm against it. Of course we must, it's an horrendous ideology, but how can we beat it if we don't even know what it is?

"The term 'fascist' can be traced back to 1914 when he (Benito Mussolini) founded the Faci Rivoluzionari d'Azione Internazionalista, a political movement whose members called themselves 'fascisti' or fascists." - Dinesh D'Souza - *The Big Lie*

Mussolini was a Marxist and member of the Italian Socialist Party. However he grew tired of the long, drawn out democratic process and yearned for a workers' revolution.

So where did Mussolini get his ideas from? Some writers like to say that he lost faith in socialism and converted to fascism but if you read the things he actually wrote at the time this is clearly very far from the truth. What he, and many others including Lenin, lost faith with was classical Marxism.

The Russian Revolution had been a bit of a shock to classical Marxists. Marx had predicted that there would be a workers' uprising in the industrialised, capitalist world. In other words, in counties such as Britain, Germany or France. But it happened in Russia and it was lead by the intellectuals, not the workers. This lead to a crisis in Marxism that would cleave it in two. As a result Marxism split into two camps, Leninism and fascism.

The French Marxist Georges Sorel (1847 - 1922) wrote that the working class needed powerful leaders to motivate them and stir them into violent action with emotional stories. Mussolini took these ideas and ran with them to create fascism.

Inspired by Sorel, Mussolini founded the first fascist party, the Fasci di Combattimento (fascist combat squad) on the 23rd March 1919. Lenin wrote to Mussolini to congratulate him.

Mussolini wrote extensively on Socialism and edited the weekly socialist publication, La Lotta di Classe (The

Class War).

"The nucleus that eventually founded fascism in Italy did not stem from the right-wing nationalists but from the transformation of part of the revolutionary left " - Stanley Payne - *A History of Fascism*

Hitler was a great admirer of Mussolini and modelled his new socialist party on the Italian fascists.

"Hitler, like Mussolini, was very much a man of the Left. Hitler too was a socialist and labour leader who founded the German Socialist Workers' Party. " - Dinesh D'Souza - *The Big Lie*

Mussolini may well have admired Lenin but Hitler did not and this was eventually to lead to his downfall. Despite being a socialist Hitler hated the Jews and he hated Russian communism. Hitler believed in the conspiracy theory known as *Jewish Bolshevism.*

Jewish Bolshevism, also called the *Zionist Occupation Government (ZOG)* conspiracy theory asserts that Jews control world politics and that Jews were behind the Russian Revolution and held the primary power among Bolsheviks.

So in the 1930s, Nazi Germany and the Soviet Union could not form a formal alliance. Hitler labeled the Soviet Union an *infernal abomination* governed by *Jewish tyrants.*

The Soviet press reciprocated with claims that Hitler was *possessed by a demon* and Nazism would *drown in its own blood.*

The Munich Agreement (September 1938) was a huge own goal for the free world. It was an attempt to appease Hitler.

The major powers of Europe, excluding the Soviet Union, agreed a settlement permitting Germany to annex a portion of Czechoslovakia. The deal infuriated both dictators. Hitler commented to an aide, *that Chamberlain fellow has spoiled my entry into Prague.*

Meanwhile, Stalin, whose representatives had been excluded from the conference, feared the British and French had *cut a deal with Hitler at the Soviets' expense.*

The following year Hitler and Stalin began to seriously consider the benefits of working together. For Germany, a non-aggression pact would guard against a war on two fronts, at least until Hitler was ready. The pact also made provision for an exchange of German technology for much needed Russian raw materials.

The Soviets thought that Poland would serve as a buffer zone against any future German expansion.

The fate of the world was sealed by the stroke of a pen on August 23, 1939.

They also signed a second, secret agreement that carved

up eastern Europe between them. If you are interested in learning more about this I recommended the book *Devils Alliance: Hitler's Pact With Stalin, 1939-1941*, by historian Roger Moorhouse .

In fact, the Nazi-Soviet Pact as the kick-off for World War II is probably the most surprising scenario that anyone could have imagined - Moorhouse says.

That's how you have to view it from the perspective of August 1939. The world was absolutely dumbstruck by this deal.

Those twin agreements set the stage for the start of World War II. Within days of signing the pacts Hitler invaded Poland. Britain and France declared war on Germany. The nightmare had begun.

A couple of weeks later, the Soviet Union invaded Poland from the east to grab its share of the spoils. In 1940 it followed up by occupying Estonia, Latvia, Lithuania and the Romanian province of Bessarabia.

Post-war writers have gone to some trouble to claim that the USSR was on the side of the Western allies during WWII. This is a very superficial view.

The fact is that the U.S.S.R. co-operated with Nazi Germany during the early years of the war in a joint effort to defeat capitalism. The Soviets only swapped sides when the *honour among thieves* pact broke down in territorial disputes.

105

A key part of the Nazi-Soviet Pact was economic: Germany agreed to swap military technology for a steady flow of Soviet raw materials. However, Soviet annexation of the Romanian province of Bessarabia at the end of June brought the Red Army close to Romanian oilfields that Hitler deemed vital to his war effort.

To smooth over some of the frustrations and to sort out territorial questions, Joachim von Ribbentrop, the Foreign Minister of Nazi Germany, invited Vyacheslav Molotov, Chairman of the Council of People's Commissars of the Soviet Union, to Berlin for talks in mid-November of 1940.

Believing the war was nearly over, Hitler wanted a broader delineation of *spheres of influence* than had been previously agreed. Ribbentrop and Hitler talked with Molotov about dividing up the *bankrupt estate* of the British Empire. At one point, Hitler stated, *let's divide the whole world.*

Molotov demanded territory in the Balkans and the Black Sea.

Hitler and Ribbentrop tried to get the Soviets to look to British India and the Persian Gulf for territorial gains.

Operation Barbarossa was the code name for the invasion of the Soviet Union by Nazi Germany which kicked off on Sunday, 22nd June 1941.

Hitler had always planning to conquer the western Soviet Union so that it could be repopulated by Germans. He also wanted to use Slavs as a slave-labour force and to seize the oil reserves of the Caucasus. Despite their close political aims, Hitler had only been stringing Stalin along. After all, in Hitler's deranged mind, the Soviet Union was being run, behind the scenes, by the hated Jews.

Hitter was obsessed with the Jews. In truth he hated all non-Arians, including the people of the Mediterranean. Had he won the war he would have turned on Mussolini just as he had betrayed Starlin.

Hitler needed a legal basis for his racism and that included an international precedent. It's interesting to note that when the Nazis got together in Nuremberg on 15 September 1935 to pass Germany's anti-Semitic and racial laws they began the meeting with a thorough examination of America's race laws.

It should be of no surprise that the Nazi National Socialists found what they were looking for in laws passed by American socialists.

Dinesh D'Souza, in his illuminating book *The Big Lie* states that "*Every segregation law in the South (southern states of the USA) was passed by a Democratic legislature, signed into power by a Democratic governor, and enforced by Democratic sheriffs and Democratic city and state officials. Most anti-*

miscegenation laws were passed in Democratic states....

"The Ku Klux Klan was a creation of the Democrats and served for thirty years as the terrorist arm of the Democratic Party. ....

"The early Klan killed as many white Republicans as they did blacks."

Since the war there has been a concerted effort by left-wing writers and activists to paint a very different picture of history.

Fascism started out as an Italian socialist, left-wing movement and its core principles of heavy handed centralised control, suppression of free speech and incarceration of dissidents still typify the far-left approach to politics.

The propaganda of the last eight decades or so has been that fascism and the communism are opposite ends of some straight line model of politics but nothing could be further from the truth. The fact is that fascism and communism are cousins, very close cousins indeed.

So where does all this leave white supremacists, neo-Nazis and the Far Right?

Part of the big fat lie, in recent years, has been to conflate those three very different political groups. The Lame Stream Media like to label people they don't understand, and are too lazy to try to understand, as *far-*

right. This includes nationalists committed to defending their countries and their cultures from being overrun by newcomers who have no intention of fitting in. The media and so-called 'progressive' educators will try to tell you it's somehow 'racist' to criticise newcomers no matter how badly they behave. Clearly these people are pushing a racist definition of racism. Clearly the same standards should apply to everyone regardless of race, religion or gender. I cover this subject in more detail in another chapter.

In Britain and Europe this group of nationalists also oppose being ruled over by the totalitarian, globalist European Union. Of course the word *nationalist* can be used in many different ways so it's important to note that throughout this book I am just using the term to mean the opposite of *globalist.*

As nationalists the so-called far-right totally reject globalism in all its forms. True nationalists support their country and it's citizens, regardless of race, religion or gender.

True Nationalists also support absolute freedom of religious belief and freedom of religious practice within the limits set down by law. They oppose political Islam because it is anti-democratic and they oppose illegal Islamic religious practices such as gender inequality, FGM, the rape of infidels and the murder of apostates.

They are totally opposed to white supremacy which, as we have seen, is rooted in Nazism, which grew out of

Marxism. White supremacists are, politically speaking, alt-left.

Of course there really are neo-Nazis groups with their pictures of Hitler, straight arm salutes and left-handed swastikas. Neo-Nazis should be placed where they belong, on the extreme left, further left even than Communists, yet conventional *progressive* thinking puts them on the far-right. This is crazy.

They will tell you that the Nazi economic system involves state control of privately run businesses whereas communism involves taking businesses into public ownership. This is true of course but it ignores the fact that although the economic ideology is different, the political one is not. Both are heavy handed systems that rely on suppressing the human rights of citizens.

Street groups such as Antifa claim to be anti-fascist but in reality they are the new fascists, indistinguishable in their methods from Hitler's Brown Shirts or the Blackshirts of Mussolini and Mosley.

It is sad that the rank and file members of Antifa actually believe that they are fighting fascism. They have been brainwashed, indoctrinated and conned by a biased and corrupted education system that has actually taught them that fascism is right-wing.

What is worse is that some of these people actually went to university and should know better. Tragically, rather than being taught how to think they were taught what to think. They were even encouraged to no-platform any speaker who might have challenged their indoctrination.

So any opposition to totalitarianism today must be aimed at educating people who consider themselves to be far-left. They must be made to respect free speech and open debate on all topics. They must be taught that it's okay to ask questions and to be critical of dangerous ideologies. Sorry Antifa but fascism can never be defeated by your hatred and violence. Only light can dispel darkness.

Social Darwinism - The big lie was arguably the brainchild of Richard Hofstadter. In his 1944 book, *Social Darwinism in American Thought* he makes a fairly shaky connection between Darwin's concept of the survival of the fittest with laissez faire capitalism.

From this Hofstadter postulated that since Social Darwinism was the basis for the Nazi eugenics programme, and since laissez faire capitalism is a right wing concept, then the Nazis must have been on the political right.

What this socialist writer and former Communist Party member conveniently forgets to mention is that eugenics was invented in Britain by Frances Galton and implemented in a big way in America before being adopted in Germany.

In America eugenics was championed by *progressives* such as Margaret Sanger, Kermit Gosnell, Charles Davenport and Harry Laughlin.

Don't you just laugh at the way socialists like to refer to themselves as *progressives* as if the world was destined to *progress* towards socialism? It's a bit like Jehovah's Witnesses calling their teachings *The Truth*. Maybe it is and maybe it isn't but calling something *the truth* or *progressive* doesn't automatically make it so. Nobody with the ability to think is fooled by such language.

Needless to say the big fat lie was seised on by *progressive* academics, taught in schools and universities and is now believed by 99% of the western world. Everyone knows the fascists and Nazis were right wingers. Only they weren't. But left or right, the point is that they were both totalitarian.

It's absolutely essential to get the truth out to people. It's the only way to stop history repeating itself. We see more and more of our rights and freedoms taken from us every day by totalitarian governments claiming they are protecting us from fascism.

The biggest of these precious freedoms is freedom of speech. We must speak out now, while we still can, before it's too late.

By now there should be no doubt in your mind that fascism and Nazism are extreme left-wing ideologies, at least according to my own model of politics. However some people, a few, with left-wing leanings, who think the left are the good guys, have written in to accuse me of saying that fascists are the good guys by association.

This is the exact opposite of what I am saying.

Fascists and Nazis hold very dangerous ideas indeed. So do the more extreem *progressives* who embrace fascist or Nazi ideas and methods, often without even realising it . I am not attacking anyone here, just their ideas.

Today's fascism is different from that of Hitler and Mussolini in so far as at least the original ones had the decency to call themselves fascists and Nazis. This modern lot have the cheek to masquerade as *anti-fascists* and gullible people are being taken in by their big fat lie.

It's bazar. The very people who are championing the heavy handed centralised state, oppose capitalism, have zero tolerance of dissenting views but rather encourage cultural intimidation, censorship (political correctness and no-platforming) and even street violence (Antifa) are claiming to be anti-fascists. It's unbelievable. All these things were fascist policies.

Even more crazy, they have got us all believing that the supporters of limited government, individual rights, a free market economy, free speech and open debate are the *far-right* fascists. Nothing could be further from the truth. All these things were hated and despised by the Nazis and fascists.

It's all backwards. It's what George Orwell called *newspeak*. I'm not referring to any specific political party here, nor to left-wing politics in general, but to the generic *progressive* left. Indeed, at least in Britain, we see these traits in both the main parties. It's time for something different.

I said at the beginning of this book that my solution is neither left-wing nor right-wing but that I am drawing wisdom from both. I have not deviated from that. However if I am to take the good wherever I find it I must also highlight the bad wherever I find it and fascism is very, very bad indeed.

Orwell knew what was coming and he tried to warn us. If only we had listened. Are we listening yet?

We must learn the lessons of history and not repeat the mistakes made by the people of pre-war Italy and Germany. Hitler and Mussolini could have been stopped had the people acted quickly enough. But they were too slow and too timid to realise that this was not going to be politics as usual.

And what the *progressive* fascists are attempting now is not politics as usual either. We must act fast. First we must get this message out so people know the truth. Then we must smash the tools they are using to enforce their conformity of thought, such as co-called *political correctness* and no-platforming. Surely it must be obvious to anyone capable of independent thought that in a freedom loving democracy *political correctness* is an oxymoron.

Finally we must thwart the globalist elite who really pull the strings behind the scenes. The politicians we see and vote for are little more than puppets.

The great totalitarian con truck has been to make us believe that fascism is the opposite of communism. IT IS NOT. Both communism AND fascism are totalitarian systems, just different masks on the same totalitarian face.

So instead of being anti-fascist or anti-communist how about coming together to become anti-totalitarian!

Let's stop squabbling among ourselves and oppose the real villain, totalitarianism.

What do the Globalist New World Order and organised religion have in common?

SUBMISSION - most world religions demand Submission, submission to their authority. Similarly under the New World Order we would all have to SUBMIT to the will of their totalitarian world government.

I most certainly have nothing against religious people, most of whom are decent folk like anyone else. I am not talking about any people but about their ideology. If a religion imposes laws or restrictions upon its followers that's a purely private matter between the religious hierarchy and the congregation. I can respect that. What I cannot accept, and neither should you, is when overzealous devotees try to impose their rules upon non-believers.

The situation gets even crazier when, for historical reasons, religion and state are intertwined. Then religious obedience gets mixed up with obedience to the state. In this sense God becomes a mask, a disguise, for Big Brother and high office within the clergy bestows political power.

When religious institutions work too closely with the state, there can be no escape from their tyranny. We only have to remember the Spanish Inquisition when people were no longer allowed to hold their own opinions.

And it's happening again now where foriegn religions, one in particular, have colluded with our government to impose so-called *hate speech* laws and political correctness. Make no mistake, these so-called *hate crimes* have nothing to do with hate. We are living in crazy times when people no longer know the difference between *hate* and *criticism*. Criticism is not hate, it's feedback, and we should all be very grateful for it.

The thought police are already watching our social media accounts, closing them down and in some cases, putting us in prison for having opinions which stray outside permitted parameters.

SUBMIT, SUBMIT, SUBMIT.

Thinking for yourself is dangerous. Resistance is futile. Big brother is watching you.

116

Well to hell with that bollocks!

There is another way.

The time has come to set ourselves free from the totalitarian globalist elite. Who's with me?

I just want to repeat here that I am not having a go at individual worshippers. We are all entitled to our beliefs. The extremists among them are being used by the globalists to destabilise the West and get us used to the idea that we must submit. These people are victims too, pawns in a much bigger game far beyond their comprehension. There are good and bad in all groups and anyway, my intention here is to discuss political ideas, not religious ideas, and most certainly not the people who hold those ideas.

I will defend everyone's right to freedom of religious belief and freedom of religious practice within the limits set by the law of the land. But when a group, any group, tries to change laws it is practicing politics not religion and in a democracy any political ideas are fair game for criticism.

Nationalism or Anarchy? - after all this talk of nationalism and anarchy you must be wondering which system I am advocating in this book. My ultimate dream is to live in a totally free, anarchist world where people are motivated by love not fear. Let's not lose sight of the theme of this book, Love Not Fear. Anarchy cannot succeed where there is fear so first we will have to find ways of getting the fear out of society and out of politics.

We can get there and I suggest plenty of ideas in this book to help get us there. One of the major sources of fear in the world today is globalism and the threat of a totalitarian world government over which we would have no control. Nationalism - free, independent nations cooperating together - is the antidote to globalism.

So to answer your question, I see nationalism as a necessary stepping stone on the path to anarchy. We can build a better world, where free people no longer depend on any government. I long for that day. But first we must learn to live with love not fear in our hearts and to do that we have to stop doing the things that scare the shit out of each other. We must consider the feelings of others. We must learn to derive more pleasure from giving than receiving. We must learn to be excellent to each other, in every situation. That's the only way we can create our utopia.

As I keep repeating, because it's important, hurt people hurt people and frightened people frighten people. We must break that vicious cycle but like nuclear disarmament, everyone wants it but no one wants to take the risk of going first. No one wants to put the needs of others first in case no one reciprocates and they are left without. Going first is to leave oneself vulnerable. This is why, in a later chapter, I suggest setting up local groups to practice these principles in a safe environment.

WOKE or AWAKENED?

Before I close this chapter let me briefly clear up any confusion you may have between the terms *WOKE* and *AWAKENED*. A lot of people think the terms are synonymous whereas in truth they are quite different (over and above the bad grammar).

There are a lot of beautiful souls, well meaning people, rallying behind slogans such as *we are all one* and *one race, the human race*. These are noble sentiments and I commend their vision. I really do. These are good people, mostly. I too want to build such a utopian world, eventually. I too am committed to working towards such a future.

But there are dark, sinister forces at large in the world working to exploit such idealism for their nefarious purposes. These forces are plotting to bring about a totalitarian world government, sometimes called The New World Order. Having strong anarchist leanings, it pains me to have to admit that the best defence we have against the New World Order is our present network of free, independent nation states. At least for the mime being.

Which beings me back to the idea that we are all one. Yes we are, but we are also individual expressions of The One. That's why globalist one-size-fits-all solutions don't work.

The reality is that we stand at a fork in the road. We are living in a world comprised of some 200 independent nations.

One fork will lead us through the land of ever smaller, more accountable nation states, 200 becoming 400, becoming 800, becoming 1600, loosing power each time until they eventually dissipate, resulting in the anarchist utopia we dream of where decision making is local and cooperative. This is the *Awakened* route.

The other fork leads us away from that, into a dystopian *progressive* nightmare where a totally unaccountable world government imposes one-size-fits-all policies on us all. This is the *Woke* route advocated by George Soros, Bill Gates, the Rothschilds et al. Like I say, most *woke* people are well meaning, beautiful souls who have no idea that they are being used by the globalist elite.

Both camps want to unite the world but one wants increasing freedom whereas the other wants to unite the world under the iron grip of the 1% of the 1%. Don't be taken in by the globalist propaganda. Please choose wisely in the knowledge that once enslaved, we will have no escape.

Choose wisely my friends.

CHAPTER EIGHT - Truth

"There is an elite in politics, in the police, in the legal system, in the media too, that colludes together to exercise power over ordinary people. .... you have to fundamentally rebalance the system .... to give ordinary people the ability to get truth and justice when they need it."

- Andy Burnham MP talking about the Hillsborough cover-up on BBC TV, April 2016.

We are drowning in a sea of lies. Our politicians lie to us, our news media lie to us, sales people lie to us, our friends and family lie to us. What hope have we of ever knowing what is really going on unless we all stop lying to each-other?

Wars are seldom about what they appear to be about. Only the foot solders believe that. The politicians and generals are just after power and world leaders may allegedly be in the pay of the international arms dealers.

POST-TRUTH is the latest new term to be added to the Oxford English Dictionary. It was named 2016 Word of the Year. It refers to the way that emotive arguments often carry more weight than facts in media coverage, elections and debates. The term came to prominence during the EU referendum in the UK and the 2016 presidential election in the USA.

In both the UK and USA campaigns, both sides were accused of spreading disinformation and lies. All the candidates were accused of telling lies and half truths and so were the news sources that supported them.

Another recent example of POST-TRUTH or POST-FACT was when Labour MP and former Mayor of London, Ken Livingstone claimed that Hitler supported Zionism because the Nazi government signed the Haavara Agreement, which facilitated the relocation of Jews to Palestine in 1933 before the Third Reich turned to mass murder and extermination. The agreement allowed a portion of Jewish emigrants' possessions, which they were forced to hand over before they left Germany, to be re-claimed through transfers to Palestine as German export goods.

Livingston probably got the details of the Haavara Agreement wrong, and the conclusions he drew from it were controversial and unsound, but nobody seems interested in looking into that. I am no fan of Ken Livingston but nevertheless, I find it strange that the Labour Party and the media kept bleating on about all the people he *offended* without once asking wherever or not he was telling the truth . Indeed, at the time of writing, he is still suspended from the Labour Party.

Guess that's just par for the course in post-truth Britain. The Labour Party couldn't give a monkey's whether he told the truth or not. All they cared about was whether is was likely to lose them votes. And the media just did what the media always do, report any old bollocks in order to sell papers.

We live in a crazy world where we expect our politicians to lie to us. We have become so accustomed to it that we now accept it as normal. And of course, the press are lying to us as well. With very few exceptions, even when they tell us the truth they only tell part of the story, the part that supports their own political bias.

In his book, Camera Assassin , my good friend Ian Cutler, tells of how he used to fake stories for the News of the World.

A more recent example of POST-TRUTH was the BBC's coverage of the post-truth story. In their report they blamed only the LEAVE and the TRUMP sides of telling lies when clearly REMAIN and CLINTON were equally guilty.

Websites such as The National Resource in the USA and several East European sites, supported by advertising, have been making money by telling sensational lies to lure in visitors and thus revenue. Over the past year, the Macedonian town of Veles (with a population of just 45,000 souls) has been the epicentre of the fake news explosion. Locals, mostly young people, have launched at least 140 new websites with American-sounding domain names such as WorldPoliticus.com, TrumpVision365.com, USConservativeToday.com, DonaldTrumpNews.co, and USADailyPolitics.com. They make their money by enticing internet surfers in with sensational and blatantly untrue headlines.

Lies, so many lies, and even lies about lying. Ever since the 2016 EU referendum, Remainers have been falsely accusing Leavers of lying on the side of their campaign bus. The Vote Leave campaigners toured the country in a red bus bearing the slogan 'Let's give our NHS the 350m pounds the EU takes every week'. Remoaners keep banging on about broken promises but what part of the word 'let's' do they not understand? The wording clearly said 'Let's' not 'We will'. It was a suggestion not a promise. Indeed Cameron was still Prime Minister and he supported the Remain side. So clearly none of the Vote Leave people had the authority to make such a promise. It was clearly just a suggestion. Of course many things were said that should not have been and the figure of 350 million pounds was probably an exaggeration.

Fake News Alert

Fake News Tip #1) - whenever you see left-wingers labeled *progressive* while right-wingers are dismissed as *populist* you know you are reading propaganda.

Fake News Tip #2) - whenever you see a government being called a *regime* you know you are reading propaganda.

Fake News Tip #3) - if you see anyone making a case to travel to a foreign country to kill people, you know you are reading propaganda.

There are things that people do not know and they don't even know that they do not know.

I have been researching this subject of many years. What really is going on? Who really is pulling the strings? How much of what we read in the newspapers or view on our television sets can we really believe? How much of our fictional entertainment is deliberately geared to moulding our beliefs, attitudes and opinions? And who is doing the moulding?

My eyes were opened a few years back when I met a former News of the World photojournalist, Ian Cutler, who confessed to me all the fake stories he had made up in the pub. Even more shocking was the revelation that his boss, Rupert Murdoch, had published the stories knowing full well that they were a pack of lies. Murdoch even said to Cutler "Its is only f**king entertainment anyway".

Another of my books, *Rupert Murdoch's Hitmen* looks into the often sordid relationship between politicians, the media, organised crime and big multinational companies. It asks many questions. You may not accept or agree with everything presented in it but it will most certainly set you thinking. You have a choice about what to believe, and the responsibility to choose wisely, in the knowledge that your choice will have consequences. In a world so full of lies and liars, how can any of us know the truth, or who, if anyone, is telling it?

Certainly not me. I didn't write that book to give you all the answers but merely to prompt you to ask the questions.

The term 'POST-TRUTH' seems to be making a value judgement. It seems to be saying that people should react more with their heads than their hearts. But how?

In a world were we are all drowning in a sea of lies and half truths, how can we ever know what is really true? How can we ever know who to trust?

Only if every single one of us makes a firm commitment can we move towards a more truthful world. Only if we all stop telling lies, even little white ones. Only if we determine never to buy a newspaper that is caught lying. Only if we determine never to vote for any political candidate who is caught lying. One strike and they are out. Only that way can we build a better, more truthful world.

Of course we must make allowances when people make genuine mistakes. Of course we must. But we must not tolerate those who deliberately try to mislead us.

We can build a better, more truthful world where no one ever need fear they are being conned or lied to. We can start to build that world today by adopting a zero tolerance approach to anyone and everyone who deliberately lies to us, whether family, neighbours, advertisers or politicians. Let's do it.

CHAPTER NINE - Absolute freedom of religious belief

for all adults and an understanding that children are not to be indoctrinated into any religion. They can decide which, if any, to follow when they grow up.

We all have the right to express ourselves freely and hold our own opinions, even if our views are unpopular or could upset or offend intolerant people. We also have the right to change our religion or belief at any time. Indeed under Article 9 of the Human Rights Act 1998 in the U.K., freedom of thought and conscience, as well as religion or belief is enshrined in law. Many other countries, as well as supranational bodies such as the European Union, have similar provisions.

In Utopia everyone will enjoy total freedom of religious or spiritual belief PROVIDED that they give everyone else that same freedom and that they obey the laws of the country in which they live before any religious laws.

You are only entitled to the same freedoms that you are willing to give to everyone else, including members, and ex-members of your own religion.

Of course religious belief is not necessarily the same thing as religious practice. Here the law of the land must take precedence. As an extreme example which proves the principle, human sacrifice is no longer tolerated anywhere in the world as far as I know and killing apostates is totally unacceptable in any truly civilized nation. Although killing people because of their faith was once common in Britain and Europe, it is now illegal almost everywhere in the world.

The last person executed for witchcraft in Britain was Alice Molland, hung at Exeter in 1684. Unfortunately religious killings continue to this day, albite illegally. One of the most famous cases in the U.K. was that of Asad Shah, a Glasgow shopkeeper, murdered in March 2016 by Tanveer Ahmed from Bradford. Ahmed, an intolerant Muslim fundamentalist, had objected to Mr. Shah wishing his customers a *Happy Easter.*

It's not just murder. There are many illegal things sick people try to get away with in the name of religion. Female genital mutilation, gender inequality, and rape are just three examples. Turning a blind eye to abuse, in the name of so-called *political correctness,* is certainly not spreading the love. It just promotes fear.

We must oppose all forms of religious fundamentalism. The truth is that there is no such thing as the one true religion. No religion has a monopoly on truth or a monopoly on God. All tolerant paths lead us into the light as surely as all intolerant ones lead us into darkness. Let your light shine forth!

Of course the right to do something in no way absolves you from the consequences of your action. If you act in such a way as to instill fear in the heart of another, don't complain when that person expresses his or her fear. Similarly when your action merely spreads distaste and loathing.

I learned this lesson the hard way when I was just sixteen. I became involved, for a brief time, with the Jehovah's Witnesses.

As you are probably aware, Jehovah's Witnesses believe that they have a monopoly on truth and that it's their duty to tell everyone about it, whether they want to hear or not.

So I went around shouting my stupid mouth off untill I lost all my friends and lost my job into the bargain. For a while I went around blaming everyone else, talking about religious discrimination and all that victim nonsense, until eventually I woke up to the fact that I had been the sole cause of my downfall. It was a bitter lesson I have never forgotten. We are all 100% responsible for the consequences of our actions.

Yes we must have Freedom of Religion. Of course we must. Nobody has the right to force his or her beliefs upon another.

Having said that I should mention that there are three

rather intolerant, overly patriarchal religions that try to suppress the divine feminine. Masculine and feminine aspects of divinity, gods and goddesses, have been revered in balance for at least 30,000 years.

Then round about the time of Abraham, maybe earlier, a shift occured. Patriarchal attitudes began to dominate and suppress the divine feminine. Priestesses who had been respected for their wisdom, understanding the cycles of life and living in harmony with them, started to be regarded as witches.

"We are living in the time of the return of the goddess. We need her wisdom to inform and inspire humanity to live co-operatively again if life on this earth is going to survive. We need her clarity of vision, her deep compassion, and her unwavering patience to live in harmony with each other and the environment."
- Lawrence Edwards PhD

As we move towards the Age of Aquarius and the utopia we are trying to build, we will find gender balance being restored. The three patriarchal religions, Judaism, Christianity and Islam will have to adapt if they are to survive, as will any matriarchal ones that have sprung up recently.

They will have to accept that men and women are equal to each-other and that God is not just male and not just female but consists of both male and female, god and goddess, aspects.

I would never try to prevent people from following patriarchal or matriarchal religions if that is their choice. I am a strong supporter of freedom of religion. I am just predicting that, as we move towards the Age of Aquarius, such religions will find themselves being left behind.

Utopia will only be possible with complete gender equality and this will have to be reflected in our ideas of divinity.

CHAPTER TEN - Universal Equality

No one thing can be equal by itself although two things can be equal with each other. This is why feminism is doomed to fail if it seeks equality for just one gender and BLM is doomed to fail if it seeks equality for just one race.

Let's have no more flotillas of little groups each demanding more rights for themselves (the me, me, me brigade) just a basic, fundamental understanding that every citizen is the equal of every other citizen regardless of race, religion or gender.

Wikipedia defines feminism as *a range of political movements, ideologies, and social movements that share a common goal: to define, establish, and achieve equal political, economic, personal, and social rights for women.* https://en.wikipedia.org/wiki/Feminism

So according to this definition, feminism is doomed to fail because it seeks equality for just one gender.

The Women's Equality Party was formed in the UK on 28th March 2015 following a public meeting in the Royal Festival Hal, London. Their Mission Statement claims *We are pushing for equal representation in*

politics, business, industry and throughout working life. We are pressing for equal pay and an equal opportunity to thrive. We are campaigning for equal parenting and caregiving and shared responsibilities at home to give everyone equal opportunities both in family life and in the workplace. We urge an education system that creates opportunities for all children and an understanding of why this matters. We strive for equal treatment of women by and in the media. We seek an end to violence against women.
http://www.womensequality.org.uk/

Note that the emphasis is strongly biased towards women's rights, NOT equality for men AND women or even between men AND women. *We strive for equal treatment of women ..... .* How can women possibly be treated equally to nobody? They can only be treated as being equal with men, and only if men are treated equally with women. Why don't they just call themselves The Equality Party? Why be sexist about it? It is the female chauvinism imbedded in the feminist movement that makes it so very hard to make gender equality possible.

We need a new approach which seeks equality for everyone regardless of gender, race or religion, a *Universal Equality Movement*. It is only by recognising that we are all equal to one and other that we can move forward into the 21st century and beyond without fear of discrimination.

But *equal* does not mean *the same*. We are all equal but

134

different and it is our differences that make us special. Social engineering stamps all over our individuality with its muddy boots. I remember a few years ago, misguided school careers advisers trying to push more girls to become engineers and more boys to become midwives. How crazy. What they should have been doing instead was to guide pupils who are interested in engineering towards engineering careers, and pupils who were interested in midwifery towards midwifery careers regardless of gender.

We hear spurious statistics in the media all the time. Only such a percentage of whatever post it happens to be is occupied by women. Well perhaps that is the same number as the percentage of women who applied. Perhaps women tend to prefer doing different things. What matters is not whether an equal number of women are following a certain career but rather whether individual people are following the careers they enjoy, regardless of gender, race or religion. Only that way can equality be achieved.

As I write this the United Nations are canvassing for a new Sectetary General. It has been pointed out that so far they have all been men and its time a woman got the job. Great, if a woman applies who is the strongest candidate, with the best experience, she should get the job. But let's not make a sexist decision here, the job should go to be best candidate regardless of gender, race or religion.

David Cameron, when he was Prime Minister of the United Kingdom, made a big deal about how many women were in his cabinet. In a post-election reshuffle, the Prime Minister promoted 12 women to senior cabinet positions making one third of all cabinet ministers female. The media, with their usual lack of taste, dubbed them *Dave's Darlings*. If you want to find evidence of sexism look no further.

Priti Patel, Anna Soubry, Andrea Leadsom, Amber Rudd, Liz Truss and others all got high profile posts. Why? Because of their experience and proven abilities? NO! Just because Cameron wanted to curry favour with the feminist lobby, that's all.

Every time you give someone special dispensation because of their gender, race or religion you set the cause of equality backwards not forwards.

We will never achieve equality this way. Biased decisions may well have been made in men's favour in the past, I don't deny that. It may still go on today in a reduced form, but, as Albert Einstein said, *We can't solve problems by using the same kind of thinking we used when we created them.*

We need to acknowledge that anti-male sexism is just as bad as anti-female sexism just as anti-white racism is just as bad and anti-black racism. Most people I speak to seem to be using a racist definition of racism and a sexist definition of sexism. We must move towards a new paradigm of Universal Equality. Jobs should never be awarded on purely sexist or racist grounds in some misguided attempt at social engineering. Jobs must go to the most suitable candidates regardless of gender, race or religion.

Morgan Freeman famously said that the best way to end racism is to stop talking about it. *I'm going to stop calling you a white man and I'm going to ask you to stop calling me a black man.* Morgan Freeman on You Tube - https://m.youtube.com/watch?v=FRnTovm26I4

I wonder if the same principle would work with gender. Perhaps the best solution is to stop bleating on about it and just quietly get on with our lives.

To illustrate the level of sexist bias in the British government, consider the Minister for Women and Equalities. Even the title is sexist. Its unbelievable. The Rt. Hon. Nicky Morgan was appointed Education Secretary and Minister for Women and Equalities on 15 July 2014. Is there a Minister for Men and Equalities? No! The very phrase 'Women and Equalities' is an oxymoron. As I said at the beginning of this article, women can only be equal to some other group, such as men, who must also be equal. Otherwise its a nonsence.

I am sure similar craziness must go on in other countries too.

Some years ago I wrote to the BBC asking whether all their radio presenters were totally oblivious to their own irony and double standards? They had run a story on the Radio 4 P.M. programme about Muirfield Golf Club in Edinburgh only accepting male members. During the programme they interviewed Maria Miller, the then Minister for Women and Equalities as well as a spokesperson for the English Women's Golf Association. They were both vehement in their condemnation of Muirfield's sexist policy. Quite rightly too in my humble opinion.

However, if its wrong for Muirfield Golf Club to exist only for men, then its equal wrong for the English Women's Golf Association to exist only for women and its equally wrong to have a Minister for Women and Equalities rather than a Minister for People and Equalities. Yet the radio presenters were totally oblivious of their own irony and double standards. (Muirfield Golf Club have now changed their policy, which is good.)

The world can do perfectly well without white supremacists, black supremacists, Christian supremacists, Islamic supremacists, female supremacists, male supremacists or any other kind of supremacists. What we need is Universal Equality, not Feminism, not Black Lives Matter, not the Ku Klux Klan and not Antifa. All these groups do far more harm than good. They have no place in the equal society we are trying to create.

Perhaps it shouldn't be automatic though. Perhaps equality should be applied for at age 18. Perhaps people should make a statement requesting to be treated as the equal of every other adult citizen and agreeing to treat every other adult citizen as their equal too, regardless of race, religion or gender. That way anyone who thinks his or her gender, race or religion places them above other people would be excluded from having equal rights.

CHAPTER ELEVEN - Race, something to be proud of

"Sometimes you look at yourself in the mirror, any mirror, and you wonder why that nose looks as it does, or those eyes--what is behind them, what depths can they reach. Your flesh, your skin, your lips--you know that that face which you behold is not yours alone but is already something which belongs to those who love it, to your family and all those who esteem you. But a person is more than a face or a bundle of nerves and a spigot of blood; a person is more than talking and feeling and being sensitive to the changes in the weather, to the opinions of people. A person is part of a clan, a race. And knowing this, you wonder where you came from and who preceded you; you wonder if you are strong, as you know those who lived before you were strong, and then you realize that there is a durable thread which ties you to a past you did not create but which created you. Then you know that you have to be sure about who you are and if you are not sure or if you do not know, you have to go back, trace those who hold the secret to your past. The search may not be fruitful; from this moment of awareness, there is nothing more

frustrating than the belief that you have been meaningless. A man who knows himself can live with his imperfections; he knows instinctively that he is part of a wave that started from great, unnavigable expanses. "
- F. Sionil José

So let's take an objective look at the reality of race and racism. Clearly there will be no place for racism in Utopia but what exactly is it and what causes it?

The Oxford Dictionary defines racism as a NOUN

1) Prejudice, discrimination, or antagonism directed against someone of a different race based on the belief that one's own race is superior.

1.1) The belief that all members of each race possess characteristics, abilities, or qualities specific to that race, especially so as to distinguish it as inferior or superior to another race or races.

Yet some people deny that different human races even exist.

More than 100 years ago, American sociologist W.E.B. Du Bois was concerned that race was being used as a biological explanation for what he understood to be social and cultural differences between different populations of people. He spoke out against the idea of *white* and *black* as discrete groups, claiming that these distinctions ignored the scope of human diversity, which of course they do.

Of course you can't distil the rich array of our beautiful human races down to just two. That would be quite absurd. However some modern thinkers, motivated by so-called *political correctness* have twisted this concept to argue that no human races exist at all. This is clearly even more absurd.

Indeed, if different races didn't exist then logically, racism couldn't exist either and I can just close this chapter now. But is it really as simple as that?

When I was at university I was taught that a species is a group of organisms capable of interbreeding within the group but not with organisms outside the group; while a sub-species or race was a taxonomic category that ranks below species, usually a fairly permanent geographically isolated group of the same species, which indeed human races were, for many tens of thousands of years, which is how they were able to diverge, evolutionally, into the different types we see today.

Members of different species can never interbreed and produce viable hybrids but members of different races can.

There is clearly a wide range of taxonomic differences in the human species (*homo sapiens sapiens*) arising from the different environmental conditions to which they become adapted. It is also true that different races were fairly permanently geographically isolated for a long time.

Skin colour is probably the most obvious of these racial characteristics. Dark skin is a protection from the strong U.V. content of tropical sunlight. Light skin enables more vitamin D to be absorbed in weak sunlight or in places where the day length is shorter.

Another obvious racial difference is broad noses in regions of the world where people benefit from being able to humidify the air inhaled through the nostrils. So many beautiful differences to be proud of.

Furthermore it is clear, from observation, that these racial characteristics are now fixed in our DNA. Individuals are capable of a very limited range of adaptation. When I lived in Spain I quickly acquired a suntan. However negros who migrate to Europe do not experience a significant lightning of the skin, even after many generations.

Preferring the company of people like us, our *own group*, is perfectly natural. We evolved that way. In our long distant past, as in modern wars, people who look different are potentially dangerous.

Not all of them where, of course, but there is a higher probability of danger from potential enemies and from people who just may not share our cultural beliefs and expectations. If the people next door dress differently from you, how much can you trust that they will act predictably in any given situation. It's all about the balance between trust and fear, and in most cases it is not conscious and it is not learnt. We come into the world hard-wired that way. Remember that this book is about enabling us to be excellent to each other by removing the causes of fear.

We can be rewired by experience of course. Trust can be build, over time, if newcomers make a real effort to fit in, and learn and comply with local customs and dress codes. But don't ever expect to be accepted into a foreign land straight away. You have to earn trust first.

Yarrow Dunham, an American developmental psychologist, studied young children's implicit preference for their own social group.

Another American, David Kelly, looked at their facial preferences.

British social psychologist, Henri Tajfel, ran a study where participants were invited to draw coloured balls from a urn. Later, while they still held the balls, they were encouraged to divide up some money. The participants gave more money to the people who held the same colour balls as they did. It really doesn't take much to get people thinking in terms of *them and us*.

But do these studies give the full picture? When I was in primary school our teacher told us that a *very special* little girl was going to be joining our class, but we mustn't poke fun of her because of the colour of her skin. We were seven, maybe eight. We had never heard of the idea of poking fun at people because of the colour of their skin. We all just looked at each-other blankly. The next day, when the girl arrived, we teased her mercilessly because the teacher had put the idea of mischief into our minds. Sometimes academics, with the best will in the world, and the best designed double blind studies, come to the wrong conclusions.

So race and racial preference are clearly a very real things but acknowledging the existence of different races is not racism. Racism is discriminating against people because of their race and this arose from a deeply held belief that some races are intrinsically superior to others.

So let's try to find out why this is so. The first thing we must recognise is that racism takes different forms in different regions of the world. As you will see, there is *true racism* and *false racism.*

Let's start by looking at the United States of America. The question of who colonised the Americas, and when, has long been hotly debated. Traditionally, Native Americans are believed to have descended from the people of northeast Asia, arriving over a land bridge between Siberia and Alaska some 12,000 years ago and then migrating across North and South America. These people, it is believed, later interbred with Vikings who had crossed the Atlantic in their ships.

145

However recent research, including a study of skulls excavated from the tip of Baja California in Mexico, indicates that the initial settlement of the continent was instead driven by Southeast Asians who had occupied Australia 60,000 years ago and then expanded into the Americas about 13,500 years ago. This would have been before the Mongoloid people arriving from northeast Asia. Even more recent studies suggest the first landings could have occurred well over 150,000 years ago.

What is absolutely certain is that Christopher Columbus did not discover America in October 1492. Rather he had arrived in an already settled and civilised country. Native Americans today like to say they rescued Christopher Columbus when he was lost at sea and if they had known the trouble he would bring they would not have bothered.

Europeans began flooding into the country to the grave detriment of the people who were already there.

The human enslavement, primarily but not exclusively of black Africans, primarily but not exclusively by white Americans, blighted the history of the United States of America in the 18th and 19th centuries after it gained independence from Britain up to the end of the American Civil War in 1865. How could people treat other human being that way? It seems quite extraordinary to us today.

The people responsible justified it with the belief they the black slaves were of an inferior race. The same excuse they used to persecute the native people. The same excuse that Arabs used to enslave white people. The same excuse Julius Caesar had used to persecute the Druids. The same excuse people have used throughout history to persecute others.

It is clear that the slave owners must have genuinely believed this lie in order to treat their slaves the way they did. So it's hardy surprising they would have brought their children up in this belief and it's hardly surprising that people still believe it generations later.

So this is the origin of white supremacy in the United States. This is genuine racism, born of ignorance and prejudice. This is what *true racism* really is.

But what of the native Americans? They may well still resent the invasion of their country by Europeans. Is this racism too? Can we really use the same term for these two fundamentally different things?

So what about Europe? What of the native Europeans? Is it legitimate for us to resent the invasion of our countries by migrants who refuse to integrate into our culture? Is this racism? Can we really use the same term for this as well?

I presented an argument earlier in this book that invasion is going to a country in order to change it whereas migration was going to a country to allow it to change you.

I began this chapter by defining racism as *prejudice,*

discrimination or antagonism directed against someone of a different race based on the belief that one's own race is superior. This definition clearly excludes discriminating again people because of the way they behave.

Moving to your country, refusing to integrate and setting up a state within a state with its own laws is clearly a very bad way to behave. I really don't think it's at all fair to classify criticising this behaviour as *racism*, do you?

Our beautiful human species is made up of lots of different races and it's our differences that make us special. I urge you to love all tolerant, broad-minded, generous people as if they were your brothers and sisters, irrespective of their origins or racial characteristics. And I also urge you to respect the native culture and people of the country where you choose to live. Only that way can we reach Utopia.

And we don't need to be the indigenous population to resent newcomers bringing unwanted changes, we just need to have been there longer. The onus is always on the newcomers to adjust to the people that were there before them, NEVER THE OTHER WAY AROUND.

If people are moving to your country, with the right attitude, please do welcome them warmly, befriend them, teach them about your culture and help them to assimilate into it.

But if they are coming with the wrong attitude, beware,

don't allow your people to end up like the native Americans, aboriginal Australians, or the native peoples of South Africa, Ghana, Zimbabwe, New Zeeland and many other places.

We can live in a tolerant, beautiful world where people are motivated by Love Not Fear, but only if we stop scaring the shit out of each other. We can enjoy the whole world, not just the bit we were born in, provided we travel and settle with respect and love in our hearts.

CHAPTER TWELVE - Maintain a stable population

The world population reached one billion people in 1804. By 1900 it had reached 1.6 billion. By 1999 it had reached six billion. Now as I write this in 2017 we stand at over 7.5 billion and rising by the second.

It is estimated that we will reach ten billion around 2083, but that will never happen. The world cannot support ten billion people. Mother Earth will have us off her back long before then, unless we bite the bullet and voluntarily limit our numbers NOW!

The bottom line is that all the things we humans are doing wrong, consuming, polluting and destroying, wouldn't matter as much if there were a lot fewer of us doing it. We are all global warmers and polluters. Please don't breed any more global warmers and polluters.

Many years ago, during the last ice age, people lived simple lives as hunter-gatherers.

In the north, on the edge of the ice sheets, they led a nomadic existence, following the herds of reindeer and elk.

Further south conditions were warmer and life was easier. A hunter could spend a day in the woods and come back to camp with enough meat to feed his family for a week. Living was easy.

At the time geologists call the Younger Dryas, some 12,000 years ago, the world warmed up, quite suddenly, and the ice sheets melted.

For those who weren't drowned in the floods that followed, life got a whole lot easier. There was more game and the people lived longer. More children survived long enough to have children of their own. The human population flourished. But after a couple of thousand years of this success there were so many people that resources were becoming scares.

Necessity being the mother of invention, the people learned how to sow crops and domesticate animals. Farming had been born bringing with it the benefits of a settled, civilised existence.

But it wasn't all good news. The strong took the best land and the weak were forced to labour in the fields of the rich. Warbands would raid each other's cattle and sheep. There was much suffering.

As society became more complex, so did our technology. The Industrial revolution saw a huge technological and sociological advance in a very short time. Good news for the rich factory owners, bad news for the new underclass, the urban poor.

But this chapter is not about workers' rights, its about population, a population that, despite wars and plague, was growing exponentially. Even two world wars had little effect on our growing numbers.

There was growing fear that we were becoming so numerous that we would soon run out of food.

Then necessity was the mother of invention once again. Scientists began work on a new miracle technique, genetic engineering.

They promised us higher yields with lower inputs. They promised us disease and pest resistant crops. They promised us a land flowing with milk and honey and we believed them.

Then came along Monasnto, a huge multinational corporation that made herbicides. They soon turned the whole GM dream on its head. Instead of developing pest and disease resistant crops they gave us herbicide resistant crops that could only be grown with the use of poisons, especially their own brand, glyphosate, also known as Roundup.

They had farmers by both balls. No longer could they save seeds to resow next season. Now they had to buy fresh seeds every year because they were patented AND they now had to buy expensive chemicals too. All to feed more and ever more people.

But its not just food. Its also pollution. Every one of us makes a mess. Every one of us fills up our dustbins or trash cans with rubbish, most of which (despite recycling) ends up as landfill. Many of us drive polluting cars. And most of us have a carbon footprint which contributes to global warming. As I have said before, I wrote the first edition of this book aback in 2017. A lot has changed since then. I am now writing these next few paragraphs in 2020, the year of 20/20 vision when things long hidden are coming to the surface.

Twenty years ago we saw how the data on Iraq's weapons of mass destruction were 'sexed up' to justify an unnecessary war. This year we are seeing governments doing the same thing with Covid data, to justify a slide towards totalitarianism. I have no doubt the same thing is happening with climate change data. But just because the figures are being hyped up doesn't mean there is nothing to it. There is a nasty bug and we are damaging our climate as well as harming our environment in a whole host of other ways too. And yes we need to do something about it quickly.

Then there is our need for housing. More people need more houses. More houses mean more agricultural land being covered in concrete. In some countries forests are cut down or other wilderness areas destroyed.

We are not the only species on this planet, nor are we the most important, but we clearly are the most destructive, the most greedy, the most dirty.

Every time we build a house on a greenfield site we are destroying some other creature's home.

Yes there are lots of things we can do, and are doing, to mitigate the damage we are doing and I have a great deal of respect for the people involved. But its too little, too late.

The cold fact has to be faced that we cannot keep expanding indefinitely on a finite planet. We just have to stop breeding. We have to find an economic system that does not depend of growth. And we have to find a social welfare system that does not pay people to have children.

If we don't find ways to control our numbers Mother Earth will do the job for us. She will find a way to have us off her back.

We can only achieve utopia with a greatly reduced human population. I am not suggesting going back to the levels we enjoyed at the birth of agriculture but we must be able to feed everyone through sustainable, organic farming.

Nature and wilderness must be allowed to return. We must clean all the plastic out of our seas and ensure that no more gets in. The same thing goes for the CO_2 in our atmosphere, as well as nitric oxides and other polluting gasses.

Mother Earth wants to make a glorious home for us and

all the other creatures we share this beautiful planet with. All we have to do is clean up the mess we have already made and then get out of her way.

As I said before, the bottom line is that all the things we humans are doing wrong, consuming, polluting and destroying, wouldn't matter as much if there were a lot fewer of us doing it.

We are all global warmers and polluters. Please don't breed any more global warmers and polluters.

CHAPTER THIRTEEN - Let's get started

So let's start loving and being excellent to each-other.
Let's start right now.

But, I hear you say, *its not easy being excellent to people who are being rotten to us.*

No its not, I quite agree. Some of us may feel up to turning the other cheek and sending love to all the takers, bigots and haters, and that's wonderful, but some of us are not quite there yet.

But if we don't start now then when? If we wait for other people to change first we will wait forever. So it may well be easier, for now, to ignore all the mean, bigoted, selfish people and just be excellent to each-other, to the people who share our dream.

There are lots of different ways we can get started. What I want to share with you here is my original idea, the one I first came up with back in the 1990s. I certainly don't intend it as any kind of diktat. It's just a springboard from which your own beautiful ideas may arise.

Back in the 1990s I wanted an island. All around the perimeter was woodland / forest / jungle.

There was a large circular clearing in the centre, several hectares, which was divided up like the slices of pizza. Each roughly triangular slice / plot was the responsibility of one named person who would be invited to build a house, a dwelling, there. That person would farm there and also carry on whatever manufacturing or other activities the person wanted to do. Perhaps the group's doctor would build a surgery or hospital there. The potter would set up a kiln and the artist a studio. The initial population of the island would have to chosen carefully to provide all essential services and a few luxury ones too.

At the heart of the circle, where all the plots convergence, was a smaller circle. This was to be the location of the municipal buildings, and the market.This would include a clubhouse where people could meet for social, as well as formal occasions such as the monthly meeting of the parliament. The group would be run as a direct democracy, rather than a representative democracy, so there would be no politicians or representatives. Everyone would speak for themselves and have one vote. Nobody would have any power over anyone else. Everything would be permitted unless specifically banned and there could never be more than one hundred laws. In order to pass a new law an existing one would have to be repealed.

Perhaps the initial ten laws could be based on the Ten

Pillars I have suggested in this book -

The Ten Pillars of Utopia

Pillar 1 - Be excellent to each-other and to the environment.

Pillar 2 - Universal Equality.

Pillar 3 - Tolerance and respect for all other broad-minded, tolerant people.

Pillar 4 - Respect our planet and all her natural systems.

Pillar 5 - Co-operation and good will between free, independent nations and free, independent citizens everywhere.

Pillar 6 - Truth.

Pillar 7 - Absolute freedom of religious belief and religious practices so long as it doesn't violate the other pillars.

Pillar 8 - Generosity - no money or barter, just freely giving and freely receiving.

Pillar 9 - Fair, people-centric, democratic government where no individual has authority over anyone else.

Pillar 10 - Maintain a stable population.

The market would be the place that everybody would bring their goods, whether manufactured or grown, to give away on set days every week

The ownership of the plots would of course depend on the temperament of the people in the group, and the wider legal environment in which the group existed. Maybe the island would come under the jurisdiction of a country and that country's laws would have to be complied with although having our own sovereign territory would of course be ideal.

I envisaged some kind of leasehold whereby the lease would revert back to the group under certain conditions, such as violation of the fundamental principles of the group as agreed in democratic parliamentary sessions.

Everyone would be eager to contribute to the best of their ability although the elderly and infirm would be totally respected. It would be sufficient for elderly people to contribute their lifetime of experience.

I understood from the very beginning that on an island, one of the biggest dangers would be overpopulation. Each plot would be big enough to support one working age adult, one elder and one child. Couples would have two adjacent plots and plots could be swapped. However, if one couple was unsociable enough to have more than two children leading to those plots being divided, and maybe divided again and divided again to accommodate successive generations, soon we would have an impoverished, starving population.

So one of the fundamental principles of the group was that plots could never be divided, although the plots could be swapped by mutual consent. So unless there was a childless couple on the island, if any couple had more than two children, then at maturity one of those children would have to leave the island. This may seem harsh, but it's the only way I can see this thing working.

The woodland would be open to everyone, a place where anybody can go to collect fire wood, or for recreation. Also, if it agrees with the founding principles of that particular group, hunting for food would be permitted there.

Of course your ideas may vary from mine, your vision may be very different from mine, and that's fine. I put my vision forward as a springboard for further ideas. I'm not putting myself forward as some kind of dictator.

So what are we actually going to do?

If anyone reading this book has an island or an estate or some other suitable piece of land I hope you will consider starting such a community.

Another approach could be to get the people together first and then to discuss ways to raise the money to buy the land. Make a list of all the skills you will need and ensure that there is at least one person in the group who can provide each one.

A third approach could be to have a location independent membership group based around a town or village where you could establish a weekly free market where members could meet to give away their produce to each other. A variation of this could be an internet based group along the lines of freecycle.org

There are hundreds of groups and communities already in existence all over the globe. Many are experiencing various degrees of government persecution. This is especially true in America. Keep going. I believe that when we reach a certain critical mass governments will fall for the same reason the Roman Empire fell, too much groundswell resistance to their tyranny coupled with the high cost of maintaining the forces of oppression.

Yes governments have their forces of oppression, police, army, national guard, but we have a powerful weapon too. One of the main ways that the Globalist Elite control us is by making us believe that we have no power to influence our own lives and the world in general.

We create our reality from our beliefs and perceptions. Second by second, minute by minute, our perceptions and beliefs are being manipulated, by media, educational institutions and by our peers.

We swim in a sea of information, except that some of us are drowning in it. Some of that information serves us well but a lot of it does not.

Our ideas about what is possible or probable for us comes from that information stream. We manifest what we think and FEEL about the most. If we are living in fear we will manifest more scary situations. When we live in love we manifest more loving, supportive situations.

So if we believe that we are powerless, we will manifest being powerless. We will fail to see the opportunities that are open to us and we will feel stuck and helpless. That experience will be our mirror. We will project our victimhood into the mirror and that's what the mirror will reflect back as us as our lives.

That's why censorship is such an important weapon for the Globalist Elite to use against us. They don't want us to see the whole picture. They must restrict our perception to the narrow band that supports the beliefs they want us to have. They want to keep us in perpetual fear, in victim consciousness.

The Globalist Elite want us to live limited lives in which we seem to be victims of circumstance. That way we look to them to solve our problems for us, problems they created for us in the first place. That's how the mouse trap works.

We get stuck in a fake feedback loop where fear makes us create more scary, hopeless situations to reinforce our perception that life is dangerous and hopeless. And around and around we go, getting ever more fearful and hopeless, until someone shouts STOP !!!

Wel I am shouting STOP right now. We are many and they are few. If thousands of us, millions of us, refuse to be censored, build our own platforms, vow to tell the truth, the whole truth and nothing but the truth, our perceptions will change and their game will be over. We can build and alternative society where we never need to fear again because we all take care of each other. Who's with me?

What we call the physical world is 99.99999% empty space. If you were the nucleus of a hydrogen atom, your single election would be several miles away.

It has been estimated that if we took all 7.7 billion people on earth, and removed all the empty space inside their atoms and between their atoms, the entire human race would fit into a single sugar cube. Just think about that.

You can never actually touch anything. All elections are negatively charged and like charges repel. The elections in your fingers repel the election in the thing you think you are touching, that's all. It's not reality.

Albert Einstein famously said "Reality is merely an illusion, albeit a very persistent one "

Sir James Jeans said "The universe begins to look more like a great thought than a great machine".

The physical world is an illusion. The hidden truth of

reality is that this is a universe built on pure energy, pure consciousness. It only appears solid to us because that's how our brains are programmed to perceive and sense it. So why do we continue to behave as if this wasn't true?

Why do we continue to use the old paradigm when trying to solve our problems and change our world? Why do we continue to fight against everything that is wrong? Mother Teresa understood this when she said "I will not participate in an anti-war rally". She understood this stuff. What we give our energy to expands, what we withdraw our energy from contracts. Fighting against a thing is to feed it energy.

The more we fight against globalism, poverty, environmental degradation, animal cruelty, corrupt politicians, injustice and hatred, the more we fuel those things.

We live in a universe of energy and consciousness. Fighting the darkness only perpetuates it because that's the way reality actually works. Our consciousness creates our physical reality.

" Hatred never ceases by hatred, but by love alone is healed. " - The Buddha

Our collective consciousness is co-creating our planet's future, moment by moment. No amount of fighting and protesting and campaigning will create real lasting change as long as there's anger and hatred and resistance in our hearts.

In the immortal words of Martin Luther King, Jr., "Darkness cannot drive out darkness; only light can do that. "

So let's stop thinking about everything that is wrong with the world and focus our attention, our energy, on the future we are trying to bring about. Focus on the utopia I have described in this book. Think about it constantly, meditate upon it, visualise it day and night. Our daily focused attention really can create a peaceful world rooted in Love Not Fear.

So how about starting a local group where you live, in your own village, town or city? Maybe you can find members through *meetup.com* or social media.

You could meet once a week to make friends and discuss how to help one-and-other. The important thing is for every member to agree to abide by the ten pillars of utopia, or at least as many of them as are piratical for a small group.

So let's make a start, right now. Let me know if you are forming a group or have formed one and I will post the details on our website and in the next edition of this book.

One great idea we can talk about in our groups is to set up Goodwill Markets where people bring the goods they have made or grown themselves. Visitors can buy the goods in the usual way but stallholders can take what they want from other stalls free of charge.

As the name implies this would require a great deal of goodwill and there would have to be a mechanism for banning persistent abusers.

There would also have to be a means of including local service providers such as the local doctor, dentist, bus company, lawyer etc., etc.

Michael Tellinger has a similar vision to my own. He wants to start with a pilot town, somewhere in the world, that can transition into a money free society.

I am a bit reluctant to recommend Tellinger wholeheartedly because some of his ideas are, in my humble opinion, a bit too far fetched. For instance he is a flat-earther, he believes that the moon is just a holographic projection and that the Mars rovers are a NASA conspiracy to hoodwink us. He could be right. Who knows? But we certainly don't have to buy into everything he says in order to benefit from his wisdom about a money-free society. He probably thinks some of my ideas are wacky too but there you go. Life would be boring if we all agreed about everything. Nevertheless, his ideas for a money free society are well worth looking into and dovetail neatly into my own.

He started his Ubuntu Movement a full 12 years before I wrote the first edition of this book, yet I did not become aware of it until two years after publication. Tellinger's idea is to start a pilot scheme in one small town or village, somewhere in the world, with the cooperation of the local mayor whereas my idea is to keep as a grass roots movement of individual people without any government involvement, not even local government. Nevertheless it certainly can't hurt to have the local mayor, and the Planning Office, on board. We both agree that we need people to set up local groups, maybe through Meetup.com, where we can talk about these issues. Anyway I strongly recommend that you take a look at Tellinger's website and sign up for his newsletter.

Tellinger's movement and mine are certainly not mutually exclusive. Let's work together to bring about a better tomorrow for us all and our descendents.

https://ubuntuplanet.org

You can find my own Towards Utopia Movement at -

https://towards-utopia.org/

Thank you. Together we really can change the world.

Be excellent to each-other
Jack Cox
Founder of the Towards Utopia Movement

CHAPTER FOURTEEN - See how far we have come

As I explained earlier in this book, we can't just turn off all the money computers today. There would be chaos. The people who hate their jobs, and that's a lot of people, would simply not turn up for work. Shops would be empty and people would starve.

We need to be a bit more cleaver than that. We need to build up to it over several years. I am writing these words in 2017. I am suggesting the Winter Solstice 2075 as Utopia Day. That will give us ten years to get this little book into the hands of millions of people worldwide, especially the decision makers, captains of industry, school teachers and university lectures. We really need to begin teaching our youngsters these principles right away.

Then we have a further 48 years for the kids starting school in ten years time to grow up and have kids of their own and for those kids to grow up.

It also gives us time for all the boring, unpleasant jobs to be taken over by machines.

If you think I am being too optimistic, that humanity can never progress so far, just look at how far we have already come.

Why can't folks just play fair and get along? If you want to start a company to make widgets you will need certain things. You will need a factory building, raw materials, machinery, design engineers, skilled workers (who are also qualified engineers) to operate the machines, accountants, administrators and managers, sales reps, cleaners and other unskilled workers. You will need all of these. If you leave out any of these people you will not be able to make and market your widgets. Its that simple. All these people are contributing, in their different ways, to the success of the company. Without them, you will be out of a job yourself. They are all essential, so why not treat them all with respect and pay them well?

The sad truth is that for thousands of years, the rich landowners, and later rich factory owners, have not been in the habit of treating poorer people well. If they had been accustomed to doing that there would not be any poor people.

Of course the people who put their life savings into starting a company, and may well work many long hours for little reward for the first few years of operation, deserve to be rewarded for their enterprise and for the gamble they took with their money. Unless there are financial incentives to start a company nobody living in our present money orientated paradigm would ever start one.

But there is a big difference between incentive and greed. Karl Marx (1818 - 1883) realised that the greatest power would inevitably be wielded by the owners of the means of production, the factory owners. Prior to the industrial revolution, the owners of the means of production had been the farm owners.

In medieval times, poor people controlled small strips of land where they grew their own food, a bit like allotment holders today. But the rich, greedy, land owners had a different vision and as they also were the politicians of the day they were in a position to abuse their power.

The Enclosure Acts were a series of Acts of Parliament which enclosed open strip farmed fields and common land, creating legal property rights to rich land owners who were effectively steeling the land from the poor.

Between 1604 and 1914, over 5,200 individual enclosure acts were put into place, enclosing 2,800,000 hectares of land. The people depended on this land in order to eat. Losing it forced them to become paid labourers. And with so many people flooding the labour market its not hard to see that individually they didn't have a lot of bargaining power. Indeed their wages were so low that they spent their entire lives close to starvation while the rich land owners grew ever fatter. Indeed this had been the plan all along.

At the beginning of this period people had been forced into near-slave labour on the big farming estates. But with the coming of the industrial revolution they ended up leaving the land altogether and sought employment in the new factories, mills and mines. As the rich land owners were the ones with all the money, they were the ones to open the factories and they brought their bad attitudes with them. They weren't all bad of course but most of them just wanted to make as much money for themselves as possible and to hell with everybody else. That meant keeping production costs as low as possible and wages were considered to be just another production cost. It never occurred to them that their workers were an essential part of the business and deserved a fair proportion of the profit they were helping to create.

Indeed it would be better not to look upon wages as a production cost at all but rather, one of the ways that profit is distributed to the people who create the wealth, on an equal footing with shareholder dividends.

As it turned out, ownership of the means of production was not the only source of power. Another was collective action and so the trade unions were born. As mentioned earlier, the rich landowners held the political power so were able to pass laws to suit themselves. As a result, collective bargaining had been outlawed as far back as the 14th century with The Ordinance of Labourers (1349). Some 400 years later the Combination Act (1799) banned trade unions and collective bargaining by British workers.

Arguably the first modern union in Britain was the The General Union of Trades (also known as the Philanthropic Society) which was founded in 1818 in

Manchester. The factory owners / politicians were not happy about this so they passed the Combinations of Workmen Act (1825) to further prohibited trade unions from attempting to collectively bargain for better terms and conditions at work, and suppressed the right to strike.

There is no doubt that the unions were needed and did a good job in protecting worker rights. However, as is so often the nature of things, they themselves grew very powerful, some would argue too powerful.

Power corrupts and absolute power corrupts absolutely. This is also what had happened with Russian communism which was originally set up to empower the people. However *the people* soon became a term euphemistically used to mean *the government* and the dream became a nightmare. The Russian Revolution had merely replaced one oppressor with another and that is not freedom.

In Britain, trade unions had begun to oppress, as well as empower their members. Closed Shops had been introduced forcing workers to join a union as a condition of gaining employment and strike ballots were far from fair or democratic. Votes were usually decided on a show of hands rather than a secret ballot. Even worse, workers who did not agree with a strike or with the aims of the union were branded *scabs* and were subject to much persecution, often violent persecution. Workers who did not vote in accordance with the wishes of the union leaders were often beaten up.

172

The right way to release the iron grip of the unions would have been to render them obsolete by enshrining worker rights in law, guaranteeing fair wages and safe working conditions. Instead the government tried to break them. Battle lines were drawn. Government intentions may have been good, to begin with, but ther methods most certainly were not and they went far too far.

Why can't people just get along? Why can't they share profits fairly, without being forced to, just because its the decent thing to do? I am sick of hearing captains of industry bleating on that they can't pay their workers more because it would make the business unprofitable. It never occurs to their blinkered minds that they can indeed pay their people more, without increasing their overall wage bill one penny, just by paying themselves proportionally less. Such a solution would not make the business unprofitable so why is it never mentioned? But successive Conservative governments didn't want a fair and equitable solution for all, they just wanted to hammer the unions.

Flying pickets or *secondary pickets* are groups of strikers who move from one workplace to another to picket there. Usually flying pickets are illegal in Britain - you can only join a picket line at your own workplace although trade union representatives can be on picket lines at different workplaces if they're responsible for organising workers in those workplaces. The practice of secondary picketing was banned in the 1970s while Ted

Heath was Prime Minister.

The first ever national building industry strike was held in 1972. Working conditions on building sites were second only to coal mines for fatalities and serious injuries. Basic facilities which people took for granted in factories, offices and shops were scarce or non-existent. There were hardly any (or no) toilets, washbasins, or lockers, let alone canteens.

Ricky Tomlinson (born1939, former building worker, now an actor, comedian and activist), remarked *McAlpines looked after their horses better than the workers on their sites.*

Fatal accidents were hardly a rarity.

Number of fatal accidents in construction reported to Health & Safety Commission (HSC), enforcement and other authorities 1971-75:

1971 -- 201 people died needlessly on building sites
1972 -- 190 people died needlessly on building sites
1973 -- 231 people died needlessly on building sites
1974 -- 166 people died needlessly on building sites
1975 -- 182 people died needlessly on building sites

All these people died because bosses put profits before peoples' lives. Something had to be done.

Tomlinson was one of the *Shrewsbury 24*, a group of 24 flying pickets who were arrested during the Builders Strike in September of 1972, while Ted Heath was still Prime Minster.

Five coach loads of pickets visited Shropshire to protest against poor working conditions in the building industry. Five months later on 14th February 1973, 24 of the pickets, including Ricky Tomlinson, were arrested and charged with over 200 offences. The charges related to picketing in the Shrewsbury area on 6th September 1972. They included charges of unlawful assembly, intimidation and affray. Six of the pickets were also charged with conspiracy to intimidate. None of the pickets had been cautioned or arrested during the strike.

There had been around 70 police officers shadowing the pickets at all times. No complaints were made to the unions or laid against the pickets at the time.

Several separate trials further and after several different convictions, the pickets always denied they were guilty of any of the charges which were levelled against them. For 40 years they have maintained that there was government interference in the prosecutions. The government just wanted to make examples of them.

Since its inception in 2006, the Shrewsbury 24 Campaign has subsequently sought for the complete release of all papers relating to the case and the arrests.

Successive governments have used Section 23 of the Freedom of Information Act (2000) to prevent the release of the papers that might shed light on any role the government of the day played in the prosecutions.

A pressure group, The Shrewsbury 24 Campaign, was formed to try to overturn the unjust prosecution of the 24 building workers.

Their main focus is an application to the Criminal Cases Review Commission (CCRC) to have these cases referred to the Court of Appeal and for these miscarriages of justice to be overturned. It was submitted on the 3rd April 2012.

The Paper Petition demanding that the Government release documents relating to the conviction of the men was served at Number 10 Downing Street on Monday 16th December 2013. The petition lead to a parliamentary debate which was held on 23rd January 2014. It was was won by 120 to 3.

Have you ever noticed the media bias in the way industrial deputes are reported? Even the left wing papers like *The Mirror* and *The Guardian* unconsciously follow this trend but Murdoch's *The Sun* and *The Times* (and *The New of the World* in its day) are quite blatant. They write about the Steel Workers' Strike or the Miners' Strike, like its all one sided and the workers are to blame for bringing the country to a standstill.

Strikes do not happen in a vacuum. They are not caused by the workers or by senior management alone. Rather they are caused the the failure of both sides to agree on certain matters. It would be fairer to refer to the Steel Industry Dispute or the Mining Industry Dispute.

Ok, they may often just be disagreeing on what constitutes decent wages but they are just as likely to disagree on vital matters of safety. Since the earliest times, manual workers have been considered to be expendable. Working class lives don't matter.

One day soon there will be no more money, the whole divisive concept will be consigned to the history books along with greed and selfishness. In the meantime we need to find a way to reduce the income gap between business owners and their employees, without reducing incentives to start businesses or to rise within them.

One good idea would be to replace Income Tax with a Differentials Tax.

Income Tax rates 2016

The Standard Personal Allowance (the amount of income you don't pay any tax on) is £ 10,600

Proposed Differential Tax rates

The Standard Personal Allowance is £ 10,600 above the earnings of the lowest paid worker in the company.

Basic rate: ---------------- 20% on £ 0 to £ 31,785 above your Personal Allowance

Higher rate: -------------- 40% on earnings between £ 31,786 to £ 150,000 above your Personal Allowance

Additional rate: ---------- 45% on earnings over £ 150,000 above your Personal Allowance

The actual percentages will need to be adjusted by the treasury to ensure that same total revenue is collected overall. They should not be permitted to use this as an excuse for a tax hike.

In this book I absolutely do not want to give the impression that politicians and the media are always working against the interests of ordinary people. Far from it. Many politicians, business people, journalists and editors, of all political persuasions, have a strong social conscience. Indeed working conditions have been steadily improving, year after year, for a long time. The Labour Party and the trade unions have been working tirelessly for a fairer society. So have the other parties.

Margaret Hilda Thatcher LG, OM, PC, FRS (1925 - 2013) was a British stateswoman and politician who was the Prime Minister of the United Kingdom from 1979 to 1990 and the leader of the Conservative Party from 1975 to 1990. Politicians do like to have their scapegoats. For Margaret Thatcher, that meant the unions. She was the nemesis of the trade union movement. Indeed she managed to destroy the power of the trade unions for almost a generation. However she did bring in Enterprise Zones and an Enterprise Allowance which helped thousands of unemployed and redundant people to set up small businesses. In fact all the parties have done some good and done some harm.

The whole left, right and centre model of politics is flawed anyway. The right want a world in which ordinary people are powerless and dependant on the owners of the means of production. The left want a world where ordinary people are powerless and dependant on the government and the unions. The common denominator is people being powerless and dependant. Maybe its time for a complete rethink.

The left, right and centre model is further complicated by immigration. You would think the right wound support immigration because increased competition for jobs pushes down wages, You would think the left would oppose immigration for the exact same reason. However the opposite is often the case. Makes you think what really does motivate these people.

The usual argument put forward in support of immigration is that immigrants work hard and pay taxes. Statistics are produced to show that, on balance, immigrates pay more in taxes than they take in benefits. What this argument conveniently fails to mention is that if the immigrants weren't there, British people would be doing those self same jobs and paying that self same tax, and what is more, they would be off the dole so saving the country having to keep them in their idleness.

Short sighted leaders in industry, and in the private sector, often find it easier to import foreign workers than to train British people. This has been especially true in the National Health Service (NHS). That's why we have far too many foreign doctors and nurses and why Brexit is causing a panic within the NHS. We will just have to stop pirating workers from other countries and start training more of our own people, and we will have to do it quickly.

But Theresa May's new government is doing the exact opposite. In July 2016, just before clearing off for their extended summer holidays, the government announced their intention to scrap NHS bursaries for university students by 2017.

The plan to scrap bursaries and replace them with loans would result in trainee nurses leaving university with over £ 50,000 worth of debt yet the starting salary for a newly trained NHS nurse is just £ 21,692 per year. Just when we should be encouraging more British people into the nursing profession, Theresa May is making it even harder for them. What on earth is she thinking?!?!

The whole idea of student loans is a nonsense. I was lucky. Back in my day we got free tuition, a maintenance grant and travelling expenses. My classmates and I left university with zero debt. The country is in a pickle. The only way out of a pickle is to think our way out. The only way to do that is to help our people become better educated, not make it harder for them.

In this book we draw attention to much that is wrong in the world and ways improvements could be made but its not all doom and gloom. Very far from it. So many things are better now than when I was growing up. Some things are worse but lots of things are better. Our standard of living is better for a start.

By way of illustration of how much worse conditions were in the past, and how far we have come, let me quote briefly from a report that appeared in the New Statesman in October 2014.

It was written by Harry Leslie Smith, an RAF veteran, now in his 90s, who was born into an impoverished mining family in the 1920s.

You can read the full article here - http://ww.newstatesman.com/politics/2014/10/hunger-filth-fear-and-death-remembering-life-nhs

Over 90 years ago, I was born in Barnsley, Yorkshire, to a working-class family. Poverty was as natural to us as great wealth and power were to the aristocracy of that age. Like his father and grandfather before him, my dad, Albert, eked out a meagre existence as a miner, working hundreds of feet below the surface, smashing the rock face with a pickaxe, searching for coal.

Hard work and poor wages didn't turn my dad into a radical. They did, however, make him an idealist, because he believed that a fair wage, education, trade unions and universal suffrage were the means to a prosperous democracy. He endured brutal working conditions but they never hardened his spirit against his family or his comrades in the pits.

Instead, the harsh grind of work made his soul as gentle as a beast of burden that toiled in desolate fields for the profit of others.

My mother, Lillian, however, was made of sterner stuff. She understood that brass, not love, made the world go round. So when a midwife with a love of gin and carbolic soap delivered me safely on a cold winter's night in February 1923 into my mum's exhausted arms, I was swaddled in her rough-and-ready love, which toughened my skin with a harsh affection. I was the first son but I had two elder sisters who had already skinned their knees and elbows in the mad fight to stay alive in the days before the social safety network.

By the time I was weaned from my mother's breast, I had begun to learn the cruel lessons that the world inflicted on its poor. At the age of seven, my eldest sister, Marion, contracted tuberculosis, which was a common and deadly disease for those who lived hand to mouth in early-20th-century Britain. Her illness was directly spawned from our poverty, which forced us to live in a series of fetid slums.

Despite being a full-time worker, my dad was always one pay packet away from destitution. Several times, my family did midnight flits and moved from one run down single-bedroom tenement to the next. Yet we never seemed to move far from the town's tip, a giant wasteland stacked with rotting rubbish, which became a playground for preschool children.

At the beginning of my life, affordable health care was out of reach for much of the population. A doctor's visit could cost the equivalent of half a week's wages, so most people relied on good fortune rather than medical advice to see them safely through an illness. But luck and guile went only so far and many lives were snatched away before they had a chance to start. The wages of the ordinary worker were at a mere subsistence level and therefore medicine or simple rest was out of the question for many people.

Unfortunately for my sister, luck was also in short supply in our household. Because my parents could neither afford to see a consultant nor send my sister to a sanatorium, Marion's TB spread and infected her spine, leaving her an invalid.

The 1926 General Strike, which began just as my sister started her slow and painful journey from life to death, was about more than wages to my dad and many others. It was called by the TUC in protest against mine owners who were using strong-arm tactics to force their workers to accept longer working hours for less take-home pay. At its start, it involved 1.7 million industrialised workers.

In essence, the strike was about the right of all people, regardless of their economic station, to live a dignified and meaningful life. My father joined it with enthusiasm, because he believed that all workers, from tram drivers to those who dug ore, deserved a living wage. But for my father the strike was also about the belief that he might be able to right the wrongs done to him and his family; if only he had more money in his pay packet, he might have been able to afford decent health care for all of us.

Unfortunately, the General Strike was crushed by the government, which first bullied TUC members to return to their work stations. Eight months later, it did the same to the miners whose communities had been beggared by being on the pickets for so long. My dad and his workmates had to accept wage cuts.

This is just the briefest taste of Harry Leslie Smith's thought-provoking memoir:
http://ww.newstatesman.com/politics/2014/10/hunger-filth-fear-and-death-remembering-life-nhs

Conditions have improved so much since Harry's time,

since the first industrial revolution and since the Enclosure Acts. We must not lose that momentum. We must not allow new technology to set us back to the days when the owners of the expensive machines held all the power.

There has been an interesting meme on social medial recently. You may have seen it. It shows a lot of very rich people sitting around a table. I have seen two different versions. In one the table is laid with lavish food, in the other the is a game of Monopoly in progress. There are no table legs. The board is supported by lots of poor people bent double. The caption reads *We could spoil their game (or feast) if we just stood up*. Well now is that time, our time to just stand up.

Please don't go away with the impression that wealth is bad, it most certainly is not. It is the way our money based paradigm distributes wealth that is bad. Socialists will try to con you into believing that it is capitalism that is bad, that a society centrally planned by a strong overbearing government would be much fairer. IT WOULD NOT. That way lies totalitarianism and globalism.

What would be really, really a whole lot fairer would be to scrap money altogether. There is more than enough wealth for all of us if we just stop keeping score and start giving and not counting the cost.

We have come so far since the Enclosure Acts. We really can make this one last push to the utopian future we deserve.

Please do join me in making it happen, for the benefit of all generous, tolerant, loving people everywhere.

Thank you.

I do hope you have enjoyed this little book. If you have the Kindle or paperback version please do leave a review. Please also download the free PDF version from https://lovenotfear.uk/FreeGift.php and give it away to everyone you know, or just send them this link. You may also like to post the link on social media.

Be excellent to each-other
Jack Cox
Founder of the Towards Utopia Movement

https://lovenotfear.uk

P.S. Please like my Facebook page - Love Not Fear - https://www.facebook.com/LoveNotFear/

You may also be interested in the Love Not Fear YouTube channel
https://www.youtube.com/channel/UCMhYa2y55NDxh 2BKcmn_n7w

I am so very grateful to all of my supporters around the world. Thank you, thank you, thank you.

Appendix A - Other Groups Worldwide

Fortunately the Towards Utopia Movement is not alone in the struggle to save our world and turn it into a Heaven on Earth. Here, in no particular order, are some of the others.

Glastonbury Healing Gardens Cooperative -
http://www.facebook.com/healinggardensglastonbury/

Healing Waters retreat and sanctuary - Glastonbury -
http://www.healing-waters.co.uk/

Mark Bajerski - https://www.markbajerski.com/

Mark is a gifted psychic, teacher and all round good guy. Mark understands the concepts many call *conspiracy theories* and has a unique ability to share what he knows with love and a deep level of spirituality.

The Thrive Movement -
https://www.thrivemovement.com/

Watch the two hour Thrive Movie -
https://www.youtube.com/watch?v=lEV5AFFcZ-s

and also Thrive 2
https://ThriveOn.ontraport.com/t?orid=103021&opid=13

These are very informative and inspirational but please never allow any movie or book, including this one, to replace your own thinking. There is much in this film I love but I most certainly don't agree with all of it. Please do your own thinking

The Solari Report with Catherine Austin Fitts - to help you build wealth in ways that build real wealth in the wider economy. We believe that personal and family wealth is a critical ingredient of both individual freedom and community health and wealth - https://solari.com/blog/

Fix the World: A New Paradigm Business Model - FTW will provide the essential services necessary to implement planet changing projects and then use the profits from these projects to fund other humanitarian projects that help the needy and heal the planet. - http://ftwproject.com/

Unified Community - a free flowing content driven metasite on the wide-ranging theme of sustainability. It provides an informational networking hub of knowledge and communication. - http://unifiedcommunity.info/

Streetbank - Share things with your neighbours

The Freecycle Network - 5,297 groups with 9,091,970 members around the world, and next door to you. It's a grassroots and entirely nonprofit movement of people who are giving (and getting) stuff for free in their own towns and neighbourhoods.

Dr. Vandana Shiva - India's anti-GMO campaigner - http://vandanashiva.com/

If you want to explore these ideas further I highly recommend two books by *Mark Boyle*, *The Moneyless Man* and *The Moneyless Manifesto*.

Rupert Murdochs Hitmen is a book about media corruption and fake news by Bobby Cummines OBE, Ian Cutler and myself Jack Cox.

The Media, Police, Politicians and Corporations are lying to you. In this book London ex -gangster turned charity boss, Bobby Cummines OBE, former *News of the World* journalist Ian Cutler and myself, Jack Cox explain about this POST-TRUTH era and how you are being systemically lied.

We explore conspiracy theories, fake news, labour relations and industrial disputes.

We even look at the causes of the problems in the Middle East, how the Arabs were conned during WW1 and how their lands were carved up by the Treaty of Versailles. We follow the money and uncover the selfish motives of the people concerned. The common theme throughout this book is the role played by the corrupt media barons such as Rupert Murdoch, the central banks owned by the Rothschild family and the arms trade.

But its not all doom and gloom. We end with a look at

191

beliefs and responsibility and how by being aware, we can choose what information to allow into our minds and as a result, we can create a better future for ourselves.